The SYBEs

WORDPERFECT 5.1 INSTANT REFERENCE

The SYBEX Prompter Series

We've designed the SYBEX Prompter Series to meet the evolving needs of software users, who want essential information presented in an accessible format. Our best authors have distilled their expertise into compact *Instant Reference* books you can use to look up the precise use of any command—its syntax, available options, and operation. More than just summaries, these books also provide realistic examples and insights into effective usage drawn from our authors' wealth of experience.

The SYBEX Prompter Series also includes these titles:

The SYBEX Prompter™ Series

WORDPERFECT® 5.1 INSTANT REFERENCE

Greg Harvey
and
Kay Yarborough Nelson

San Francisco • Paris • Düsseldorf • Soest

Acquisitions Editor: Dianne King
Series Editor: James A. Compton
Copy Editor: Kathleen Hummel
Technical Editor: Maryann Brown
Word Processor: Chris Mockel
Series Book Designer: Ingrid Owen
Typesetter: Charles Cowens
Proofreader: Lisa Jaffe
Cover Designer: Thomas Ingalls + Associates

dBase III is a registered trademark of Ashton-Tate.
Hercules Graphics Card Plus, Incolor Card, and RamFont are trademarks of Hercules
Computer Technology, Inc.
IBM and PC-DOS are trademarks of International Business Machines Corp.
LaserJet is a trademark of Hewlett-Packard Co.
Lotus 1-2-3 is a trademark of Lotus Development Corp.
Mace Utilities is a trademark of Paul Mace Software.
MS-DOS is a trademark of Microsoft Corp.
Norton Utilities is a trademark of Peter Norton Computing.
PostScript is a trademark of Adobe Systems, Inc.
SideKick is a trademark of Borland International.
WordPerfect is a trademark of WordPerfect Corp.
WordStar is a trademark of WordStar International.

SYBEX is a registered trademark and Prompter Series is a trademark of SYBEX, Inc.

SYBEX is not affiliated with any manufacturer.

Every effort has been made to supply complete and accurate information. However,
SYBEX assumes no responsibility for its use, nor for any infringements of patents or
other rights of third parties which would result.

An earlier version of this book was published under the title *WordPerfect 5 Instant
Reference* copyright ©1988 SYBEX Inc.

Library of Congress Card Number: 89-90543
ISBN: 0-89588-674-X
Manufactured in the United States of America
10 9 8 7 6 5

Acknowledgments

Thanks are due to the following people: At SYBEX, Dr. R. S. Langer and Alan Oakes furnished the inspiration for this series over dim sum; among those who worked directly on this book, Maryann Brown and Michael Gross provided particularly valuable technical suggestions. At WordPerfect Corporation, Paul Eddington provided current software and documentation.

Table of Contents

Overview

The idea behind this book is simple. When you are stymied by a command in WordPerfect that does not work as you intended, or when you want a quick refresher about a certain procedure, you need a single source of information that can quickly help you solve the problem at hand and get on with your work.

This *Instant Reference* is intended to give you as quickly as possible the essential information necessary to get the most from WordPerfect's numerous features—both the basic commands and the sophisticated functions that you may not use on a daily basis. It covers versions 5.0 and 5.1 of the program. Version 5.1 has added new features, as discussed in the **Update Notes** section of this Overview.

Because we expect you to consult this book as a reference for solving day-to-day application problems, we have assumed that your copy of the program is already installed. In addition, because WordPerfect can be customized to suit individual preferences in many ways, space limitations have prevented us from discussing customization in detail. For detailed information about installation, customization features, and advanced topics such as the macro command language, see the authors' *WordPerfect 5.1 Desktop Companion* (SYBEX, 1990).

Basic Program Functions

WordPerfect is a screen-oriented word processor, which means that as you create and edit your document, it appears on your screen pretty much as it will when it is printed: What you see is what you get. As soon as you issue the **WP** startup command and press ↵, an initial startup screen appears briefly. After the initial startup screen, you will be presented with the editing screen. On it, a default *status line* indicates the document window you are in (Doc 1 or Doc 2) as well as the current page, line, and horizontal cursor position. Page breaks are indicated by a line of hyphens extending across the width of the screen.

To keep the screen view of your document as similar as possible to the printed version, WordPerfect does not display any of the special codes it uses to format the text, nor does it show any menu selections until you issue the appropriate command.

To see the formatting codes that are being used in your document, press Reveal Codes (Alt-F3); to close this Reveal Codes window, press Alt-F3 again. (If you're using pull-down menus in version 5.1, you can choose Reveal Codes from the Edit menu.) You can add and edit text while in the Reveal Codes window. In version 5.1, you can change the size of the Reveal Codes window.

Update Notes

WordPerfect 5.1 is now installed on your hard disk with a menu-driven installation program. To run it, type **install** at the DOS prompt. WordPerfect will automatically create a directory named C:\WP51 and install your files there. You will be prompted at each stage of the installation about which features of WordPerfect—such as the Speller, the Convert program, and so forth—you want to install.

You issue commands to WordPerfect by pressing the function keys in combination with the Ctrl, Shift, and Alt keys. You can select menu choices by pressing either the corresponding number *or* a mnemonic letter, which is usually but not always the first letter of the option name. In version 5.1, you can also use a system of pull-down menus and a mouse to select items. You can use any combination of typing from the keyboard, selecting from pull-down menus with the keyboard (by typing the highlighted mnemonic letter of the command), or pointing and clicking with the mouse.

If you have been using an earlier version of WordPerfect, you will find that version 5.1 has been somewhat reorganized, primarily for ease of use. As a result, some of the functions have been reassigned to different keys. If you are a previous user of WordPerfect 5.0, you may find the following quick summary helpful:

- **F1**—A new DOS Command option has been added to Ctrl-F1 (Shell). You can now execute a DOS command without exiting from WordPerfect. The Setup menu (Shift-F1) has been radically changed to include new mouse and pull-down menu display options. Also added to the Setup menu are Document Management options that support using longer, more descriptive document names and allow you to increase the scope of the Document Summary feature by assigning document types and customizing the way document summaries work. A new hyphenation dictionary has been created, and you can choose whether to use dictionary or rule methods for hyphenation. A new unit of measure— 1/200ths of an inch, for fine adjustment in typesetting— has been added. In addition, the Initial Settings submenu of the Setup menu allows for merging of delimited files; it also lets you specify how you want equations printed. Mapping options have been added to the Keyboard Layout feature, and Location of Auxiliary Files is now called Location of Files. Consult *WordPerfect 5.1 Desktop Companion* (SYBEX, 1990) for information about using these customization features.

- **F2**—This key (Search, Replace, and Speller) remains essentially the same. The Speller now checks for irregular capitalization as well as its usual functions, and you can choose dictionary-based or rules-based spell checking.

- **F3**—Help (F3) is now context sensitive, which means that you can get help on a feature as you are using it by simply pressing F3 or choosing Help from the pull-down menu. In addition, you can now size the Reveal Codes window (Alt-F3).

- **F4**—On enhanced keyboards, Ctrl-Del is now a shortcut for Move, and Ctrl-Ins is a shortcut for Copy.

- **F5**—Text In/Out (Ctrl-F5) has a new option, Spreadsheet, that allows you to import spreadsheet data into WordPerfect. You can also create dynamic links between the spreadsheet and the WordPerfect document so that as the data in your spreadsheet program changes, those changes are reflected in the document in WordPerfect. In addition, List Files (F5) allows you to display long, descriptive document names and use a new Find feature, which replaces version 5.0's Word Search feature, to locate files quickly. Shift-F5 (Date/Outline) has a new Outline feature that allows you to work with "outline families"—groups of related entries in an outline. You can also create outline styles. Mark Text (Alt-F5) renames version 5.0's Automatic Reference feature Cross-Reference.

- **F6**—The functions of this key remain essentially the same, although in WordPerfect 5.1 default tabs are relative, which means that they remain the same relative distance from the left margin when you change margins. In WordPerfect 5.0, tabs remained an absolute distance from the left edge of the page.

- **F7**—A new Multiple Pages option on the Print menu (Shift-F7) allows you to print selected pages from the document on the screen. Previously, to print selected pages, you had to save a document and print it from disk. Type Through (version 5.0) is no longer supported. Version 5.1 automatically formats documents that have been Fast Saved before you print them. A revised Fonts and Cartridges feature allows you to see built-in fonts and groups families of fonts so that you can select them easily. The Alt-F7 (Math/Columns) key has been renamed Columns/Tables, and a new Tables feature makes it easy to create rows and columns of data and carry out mathematical calculations on them. In addition you can place columns in graphics boxes, headers, and footers.

- **F8**—Full justification is now the default in version 5.1. In addition, you can choose between relative and absolute (version 5.0-style) tabs, as mentioned above, and tabs will move dynamically on the screen as you change them on the tab ruler line. On the Page menu, the Paper Size/Type feature replaces the Forms feature of version 5.0. In addition, the Page Numbering feature has several new options that make it easier to combine text and page numbers, which formerly had to be done in a header or footer. A leading option has been added to the Printer Functions feature. The Styles (Alt-F8) key has been enhanced to allow you to put graphics in styles, merge with styles, and use outline styles.

- **F9**—A new format for merge codes makes it easier to design a merge document. The ^F code, for example, is now replaced by Field =, and ^E has been replaced by End Record =. In addition, you can select merge commands and macro commands while creating a merge document. New merge commands let you use named fields in a document and chain and nest mail-merge files to automate merge operations. You can now place merge codes in headers, footnotes, and so forth. On the Graphics key (Alt-F9), Equation boxes have been added, and with the Equation Editor you can easily create equations on the screen.

- **F10**—New macro commands have been added to increase the power of 5.1 macros. Also, a Description option makes it easier to edit macro descriptions, and you are placed directly in the macro editor when you edit macros.

In addition, WordPerfect 5.1 comes with additional keyboards for keyboard shortcuts and equations. A new Copy-Font program allows you to copy information from one printer file to another so that you do not have to reinstall fonts each time you get an updated printer driver from WordPerfect.

The List feature (F5) now works for spreadsheet file names and ranges, for retrieving documents, and viewing graphics files.

WordPerfect 5.1 will create graphically any character that you compose, even if it is not in the font that you have selected. If your printer will print graphics, you will be able to print that character.

WordPerfect 5.1 contains many other new features. They are listed alphabetically here; for more information on any of them, refer to the appropriate heading in this *Instant Reference:*

Document Management (see **Document Summary**); Equations; Find; Labels; Leading; Mouse; Print Multiple Copies; Pull-Down Menus; Short/Long Document Names; Spreadsheet; Tables

Using This Instant Reference

Each entry in this book is designed to provide the essential information about a particular WordPerfect feature in a clear, accessible format. When you only need to be reminded of the menu sequence to follow, see the entry's **Sequence of Steps** section.

With version 5.1, you can use a mouse, pull-down menus, and the keyboard, in any combination, to carry out Word-Perfect operations. However, the main pull-down menu groups features in a different way than the traditional function-key menus. When you press Alt-= (or simply Alt if you have specified it in the Setup menu) or click the right mouse button, the following main pull-down menu appears:

File Edit Search Layout Mark Tools Font Graphics Help

You can then select from this menu in several ways:

- By typing the highlighted mnemonic letter of the item's name
- By typing the number that corresponds to the position of the item in the menu
- By clicking on an item with the left mouse button
- By dragging the mouse pointer to the item you want and then releasing the mouse button
- By pressing ↵ when an item is highlighted.

If an item in a pull-down menu is in brackets, it cannot be selected.

Once you have selected the command you want from the main pull-down menu, you may in some cases see an additional pull-down menu before you reach the regular system of WordPerfect menus. Menu options that lead to additional pull-down menus have a right-pointing arrowhead on the right.

To summarize these alternative paths in a single menu sequence that you can follow at a glance, we emphasize the name of the option you select at each stage, not the various ways you can select it. A typical sequence of steps looks like this:

Shift-F8 (Format) *or* ⌐ **Layout**

➡ **Line**

➡ **Line S**pacing *<spacing value>* ⏎

➡ **F7** (Exit)

For the sake of simplicity and because the numbering sometimes differs between versions of the software, we've omitted the numbers you can also use to select menu items; these numbers appear on the screen only when you use a function-key menu. Our step sequences use the 5.1 names and specifically note any differences in version 5.0.

The symbol ⏎ stands for the Return or Enter key. A hyphen between two keys means they are to be pressed in combination. (For example, **Shift-F7** means "Press the Shift key and, while holding it down, press the F7 key and release them both simultaneously.") Any word or phrase enclosed in angle brackets is a placeholder for some actual value you must enter (for example, *<spacing value>*).

Under the heading "USAGE," you will find a short discussion of the command or option, or in some cases, a step-by-step sequence of instructions you must follow to accomplish a complex task, such as merge-printing or creating an index. If all you need is a quick review of the step sequence that is required, you don't need to read the discussion. If you need additional information, you will usually find enough details in the discussion to allow you to accomplish the task at hand.

Finally, where appropriate, you'll find cross references to commands of related interest under the heading "SEE ALSO."

Advance

Advances the printer to a specific line or position on the page.

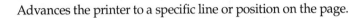

SEQUENCE OF STEPS

Shift-F8 (Format) *or* 🖰 **L**ayout pull-down

➧ **O**ther

➧ **A**dvance

➧ **U**p; **D**own; **L**ine; **L**eft; **R**ight; **P**osition

➧ *<measurement to advance>* ↵

➧ **F7** (Exit)

USAGE

The Advance feature advances the printer to a specific position on the page. To advance the printer up, down, left, or right of the current printing position (that is, the place where the [Adv] code is entered), enter a distance that is relative to the cursor's position when you use the command. To advance the printer to a specific line or column, enter a measurement that is an absolute position on the page. When using the Advance to Line option, enter the distance from the top of the page. When using the Advance to Position option, enter the distance from the left edge of the page.

To use the Advance feature, move the cursor to the place where you want the advance to begin and follow the step sequence shown at the beginning of this section. After you press F7 (Exit), type the text to be advanced.

Although the status line will reflect the advance position, the cursor does not move when you use this command. To return to the original position when using Advance Up, Down, Left, or Right, select the opposite Advance option (down if you used up, right if you used left, etc.) and enter the same distance you specified earlier. To return to the original line or column when using Advance to Line or Advance

vance to Position, repeat the advance procedure, selecting the same Advance option but entering the original line or offset position as the distance. To prevent the text from being advanced as indicated, locate the appropriate [Adv] code in the Reveal Codes screen and delete it.

The Advance feature is especially useful in layout work involving text and graphics on a page. You can use it to fine-tune the placement of headings in Text boxes and to position text that overlays other types of graphics on the page (see **Graphics**).

Append Block

Adds a marked block of text to the end of another document.

SEQUENCE OF STEPS

To append a sentence, paragraph, or page:

Ctrl-F4 (Move) *or* ⌨ **E**dit pull-down *then* **S**elect

➠ **S**entence; **P**aragraph; **P**age

➠ **A**ppend

➠ *<file name>*

To append a marked block, column, or rectangle:

Alt-F4 (Block) *or* ⌨ **E**dit pull-down *then* **B**lock

➠ *[highlight block of text with cursor keys]*

➠ **Ctrl-F4** (Move) *or* ⌨ **E**dit pull-down *then* **A**ppend

➠ **B**lock; **T**abular **C**olumn; **R**ectangle

➠ **A**ppend

➠ *<file name>*

USAGE

When you append a block of text, WordPerfect adds it to the end of a document saved on disk. You can append a discrete block of text like a sentence, paragraph, or page without marking it as a block first. When appending any other type of block (such as several words but not an entire sentence, several lines but not an entire paragraph) or a tabular column or rectangle, you must use Block to mark the text to be appended before you use Move (Ctrl-F4).

When using either method, indicate the type of block and select the Append option. You are then asked for the name of the file to which this text will be appended. Type in the file name. If this file is not in the current (default) directory, include the path name. After entering the name, press ↵ to have the text added to the end of the disk file.

NOTE

You can also append the text of a disk file to the document currently in the editing screen. To do this, move to the end of the document (Home Home ↓), select Retrieve Text (Shift-F10), and enter the name of the document whose text you want appended. The same thing happens when you use the Retrieve option on the List Files menu and have a document on the editing screen.

SEE ALSO

Block Operations; Cut and Copy Text; Retrieve.

Base Font

Changes the basic font used in printing the document from the cursor's position forward.

SEQUENCE OF STEPS

Ctrl-F8 (Font) *or* `⌐` **Fo**nt pull-down

➠ Base **Fo**nt

➠ *[highlight font] or* **N N**ame Search

➠ **S**elect; *or [double-click with mouse]*

USAGE

The *current font* represents the font in which the text is normally printed. This font depends upon the printer that you have selected and the initial font that you have assigned to it (see **Printer, Select**). To switch to a new basic font in the document, use the Base Font option on the Font menu. When you select a new font in this way, it becomes the new current font from the cursor's position forward in the document.

The current font also determines what sizes will be used when you select different font size options such as Fine, Small, or Large, or different attribute options like Bold or Italics (see **Font**). For example, if you select a new base font of Times Roman 10 point, WordPerfect will use Times Roman 10 point bold to print boldfaced text in the document, Times Roman 10 point Italic to print italicized text, and so on. Likewise, when you make a change to the size, it will use different-sized fonts in the Times Roman family, such as Times Roman 6 point for Fine, Times Roman 8 point for Small, Times Roman 12 point for Large, and so forth. The actual sizes chosen for each change in size depend upon the fonts your printer supports and the fonts you have selected for that printer. Moreover, the font choices available when you change the current font with the Base Font option are determined by the fonts you have selected for the printer you are using (see **Cartridges and Fonts**). To prevent a font change from taking place, locate the [Font] code in the Reveal Codes screen and delete it.

You can also change the base font by using the Format menu (Shift-F8) and selecting the Document option; then select Initial Base Font. Do this when you want to override *in the current document only* the initial base font selected for your printer.

Changing the base font from the Font pull-down menu, the Format menu (Shift-F8), or the Font key (Ctrl-F8) all change the base font only in your current document. To change the base font that you have assigned to your printer, see **Printer, Select**.

SEE ALSO

Cartridges and Fonts; Font; Printer, Select.

Binding Offset

Shifts text to the right on odd-numbered pages and to the left on even-numbered pages.

SEQUENCE OF STEPS

    Shift-F7 (Print) *or* ▭ **File** pull-down *then* **P**rint

➠ **B**inding Offset

➠ *<measurement for binding width>* ↵

➠ **F7** (Exit)

USAGE

You can use the Binding Offset option on the Print menu to ensure that there is sufficient room to bind the document when it is going to be reproduced on two-sided copies. To determine how far the text is shifted to the right on odd-numbered pages and to the left on even-numbered pages, you set a binding width.

The binding width is entered as an absolute measurement from the left or right edge of the paper and overrides the left and right margin settings that are in effect. You can enter the binding width any time prior to printing the document.

If you intend to reproduce the document on just one side of the paper, you can ignore the Binding Offset option; just increase the left margin setting to allow sufficient room for binding.

To remove the binding width before printing a document during the same work session, select Binding Offset from the Print menu and enter **0** as the binding width measurement.

Block Operations

Defines a block of text on which you can then perform any of a number of operations.

SEQUENCE OF STEPS

Alt-F4 (Block) *or* ⌐⊃ **E**dit pull-down *then* **B**lock

➡ *[highlight block]*

➡ *[select the operation to be performed on the block]*

USAGE

The Block command is used to highlight (mark) a section of text for use with other WordPerfect commands. Once you have marked a block of text, you can use any of the following WordPerfect features:

Align; Append; Bold; Center; Comment; Convert Case; Copy; Delete; Flush Right; Font: Appearance and Size; Format (Block Protect); Macro; Mark Text: Index, List, Table of Authorities, Table of Contents; Mouse; Move: Block, Tabular Column, Rectangle; Print; Replace; Save; Search; Shell (if using the WordPerfect Library); Sort; Spell; Style; Switch; Tables; Text In/Out; Underline.

Marking a Block

To mark a block of text, position the cursor at the beginning of the block and select Block. The message *Block on* will blink on and off at the bottom left of your screen. Position the cursor at the end of the block; as you move the cursor, the text included will be highlighted. Then select the operation you want applied to the block.

When marking the block, you have several options for positioning the cursor: Use the Search feature to move the cursor forward or backward to a particular place in the document. Press ↵ to extend the block to the next [HRt] code (hard return). Type a particular character to extend the block to that character—such as a period to include text up to the end of the sentence. Press ↑ or ↓ to extend the block up or down to include a number of lines. Press Ctrl-→ to extend the block to include several words.

Many WordPerfect commands behave differently if you have marked the text before using them. The differences are summarized in Table 1.

Marking a Block with the Mouse

To use the mouse for blocking text, select the beginning of the text you want to block by clicking and holding the left mouse button. Then drag the mouse (see **Mouse**) to the end of the selection. When the text you want to block is highlighted, release the left mouse button. You can change the size of the blocked area by using the arrow keys or the Search feature to extend the blocking to the character or word you specify.

You can also turn on blocking from the pull-down menus by selecting Edit and then Block.

Rehighlighting a Block

After you mark the block and select a WordPerfect feature, the highlighting and the *Block on* message will disappear. To

KEY	BLOCK ON	BLOCK OFF
F1 (Cancel)	Cancels block	Cancels; Undeletes
Alt-F2 (Replace)	Replaces in block	Replaces in document
Ctrl-F2 (Spell)	Checks block	Checks word, page, or document; Changes dictionary, Looks up word; Gets word count
Shift-F3 (Switch)	Uppercases or lowercases block	Switches to other window
Ctrl-F4 (Move)	Cuts, copies, moves, or appends block; Cuts/copies column or rectangle	Moves sentence, paragraph, or page; Retrieves column, text or rectangle
Alt-F5 (Mark Text)	Marks for ToC, list, paragraph numbering	Turns outlining, redline, strikeout, index numbering on/off; Enters short form for ToA; Other options define styles for paragraph and outline numbering (version 5.0), ToC, index, and lists; Deletes redline; Edits ToA; Generates ToC and lists; Generates cross references; Creates master documents
F6 (Bold)	Bolds block	Bolds as text is entered
Alt-F6 (Flush Rt)	Moves block flush right	Moves text flush right as you enter it

Table 1: Block Commands

KEY	BLOCK ON	BLOCK OFF
Shift-F6 (Center)	Centers block	Centers text as you enter it
Shift-F7 (Print)	Prints block	Accesses Print menu
F8 (Underline)	Underlines block	Underlines text as you enter it
Shift-F8 (Format)	Protects block	Accesses page format options
Ctrl-F9 (Merge/Sort)	Sorts block	Merges; Sorts; Specifies sort sequence
F10 (Save)	Saves block in new file	Saves document

Table 1: Block Commands (continued)

rehighlight the block you just used, press Block (Alt-F4) and then Go To (Ctrl-Home) twice. To move the cursor directly to the beginning of the block, press Go To (Ctrl-Home) followed by Block (Alt-F4).

Press Cancel (F1) or Block (Alt-F4) to turn off the *Block on* prompt and cancel the intended block operation.

To cancel blocking with a mouse, click outside the highlighted area. You can also cancel blocking by clicking both buttons at the same time (on a two-button mouse), or the left and right buttons (on a three-button mouse). In addition, you can use the Cancel key (F1).

SEE ALSO ════════════

Bold; Center; Cut and Copy Text; Mark Text; Save; Sort and Select; Speller; Underline.

Block Protect

Prevents a marked block of text from being split by a soft page break.

SEQUENCE OF STEPS

Alt-F4 (Block) *or* ⌐▭ **E**dit pull-down *then* **B**lock

➠ *[highlight block of text]*

➠ **Shift-F8** (Format) *then* Protect block? **No** (**Yes**) *or*
⌐▭ **E**dit pull-down *then* Protect Block

USAGE

You can use block protection to ensure that any block of text is not split between pages. If you make editing changes that would split the protected text between pages, WordPerfect will shift the entire block to the following page. This feature can be used effectively to keep tables on a single page.

To block-protect text, move the cursor to the beginning of the block, select Block, and move the cursor to the end of the block. Then, select Format, and in response to the prompt, select **Y** to have the block protected; or select Protect Block from the Edit pull-down menu.

To remove block protection, locate the [Block Pro:On] or [Block Pro:Off] code in the Reveal Codes screen and delete it.

SEE ALSO

Conditional End of Page; Page Break, Soft and Hard; Widow/Orphan Protection.

Bold

Enhances the selected text by printing it in a boldface font or with doublestrike.

SEQUENCE OF STEPS

To boldface text as you type it:

F6 (Bold) *or* ꗪ **F**ont pull-down *then* **A**ppearance *then* **B**old

➠ *[type text]*

➠ **F6** (Bold) *or* ꗪ **F**ont pull-down *then* **A**ppearance *then* **B**old

To boldface existing text:

Alt-F4 (Block) *or* ꗪ **E**dit pull-down *then* **B**lock

➠ *[highlight text]*

➠ **F6** (Bold) *or* ꗪ **F**ont pull-down *then* **A**ppearance *then* **B**old

USAGE

WordPerfect allows you to enhance portions of text with boldfacing by placing the text between a pair of Bold formatting codes. Boldfacing is indicated on the screen by double-intensity or a different color. When printing the boldfaced text, the program will either select a bold version of the font in use or doublestrike the text, depending upon the type of printer you have.

You can also boldface text by using Font (Ctrl-F8), selecting the Appearance option and then selecting Bold, or by using the Font or Edit pull-down menu.

To remove boldfacing, locate either the [BOLD] or [bold] code in the Reveal Codes screen and delete it. You only have to delete one of the pair to delete both and remove the boldfacing.

When the cursor is located on a boldfaced character in the text, the number at the Pos indicator is shown in the same attribute used by your monitor to display bold text (double-intensity or a new color). As soon the cursor is moved ahead of or behind the Bold code, this number returns to the normal attribute. Thus, you can refer to the Pos indicator to locate a Bold code for deletion without using the Reveal Codes screen.

When you are about to delete a Bold code in this way (whether intentionally or not), WordPerfect prompts you for confirmation. Select **Y** for Yes to delete—if you simply press ↵, the boldfacing will remain.

SEE ALSO

Base Font; Cartridges and Fonts; Font.

Canceling a Command

Terminates almost any WordPerfect command that is being carried out.

SEQUENCE OF STEPS

F1 (Cancel) *or [hold down one mouse button and click the other (on a two-button mouse)] or click the middle mouse button (on a three-button mouse].*

USAGE

You can use F1 or the mouse buttons almost any time you wish to cancel the command you have initiated. In certain cases, you can press the Esc key two or more times to cancel a particular command.

To back out of a menu that you have selected, you can click the right mouse button; it works like the F7 (Exit) key.

When you have not initiated a WordPerfect command, the Cancel key undeletes text. For more information about this use of Cancel, see **Undelete**.

SEE ALSO

Esc Key; Undelete.

Cartridges and Fonts

Allows you to select the fonts you want to use in the document.

SEQUENCE OF STEPS

To select fonts:

> **Shift-F7** (Print) *or* ⌨ **F**ile pull-down *then* **P**rint
>
> ➡ **S**elect Printer
>
> ➡ *[highlight the printer that uses the fonts]*
>
> ➡ **E**dit
>
> ➡ **C**artridges and Fonts
>
> ➡ *[highlight Cartridges or Soft Fonts]*
>
> ➡ **S**elect
>
> ➡ *[mark fonts with * if they will be present when job begins or with + if WordPerfect must load them during print job]*
>
> ➡ **F7** (Exit) *five times*

To designate where the soft fonts are located:

> **Shift-F7** (Print) *or* ⌨ **F**ile pull-down *then* **P**rint
>
> ➡ **S**elect Printer

➠ *[highlight the printer that uses the fonts]*

➠ **E**dit

➠ Path for **D**ownloadable Fonts and Printer Command Files

➠ *<drive/directory path>* ↵

➠ **F7** (Exit) *three times*

USAGE ═══════════════

If your printer can use cartridges or soft fonts other than those built into it, you need to select them before you can use them in your documents. The Cartridges and Fonts menu will show you the cartridges and print wheels that your printer supports and the amount of memory available for downloading soft fonts. With version 5.1 you will see built-in fonts also. In addition, font families will be grouped together so that you can select them easily. At the bottom of the screen, there are three options:

1 Select; **2** Change **Q**uantity; **N N**ame search: **1**

If your laser printer has more than 512K of memory, select the Quantity option. Enter the amount of additional memory in kilobytes above the standard configuration for your printer (512K for the LaserJet), plus the amount of memory available for soft fonts, shown on the screen. For example, if you equip your LaserJet with 1.5Mb of total memory (1Mb or 1024K additional), enter **1374** for the quantity—1024K extra memory plus the 350K currently available for soft fonts.

To select cartridge fonts, be sure that the highlight cursor is on *Cartridges* and then choose the Select option. Mark the cartridges you wish to use by highlighting them and typing an asterisk (*). Press Exit (F7) twice and WordPerfect will update the printer definition file.

To select soft (downloadable) fonts, move the highlight cursor to Soft Fonts and then choose the Select Fonts option. To quickly locate the font you want to add from the list, use Name Search by pressing **F2** or **N** and typing in the first few letters of the font name.

Move the highlight cursor to soft fonts and choose Select to display a list of font groups. Select a group, and then mark with an asterisk (*) all of the fonts that will be present (that is, downloaded) before the print job begins. Mark all of the fonts that will be downloaded during the print job with a plus (+). Press Exit (F7) three times and WordPerfect will update the printer definition file.

If you have marked fonts that are to be downloaded by WordPerfect during the print job, you must indicate the directory that contains the fonts. Note that before printing you must manually load any fonts marked with *, using the Initialize Printer option on the Print menu—then WordPerfect will download them for you. To indicate this directory, select the Path for Downloadable Fonts and Printer Command Files option and enter the complete path name.

The fonts you have selected will appear on the Base Font menu and may be used in the document either by selecting a new base font or by selecting a new size or appearance (see **Base Font** and **Font**).

To unmark fonts, repeat the procedure for editing the fonts for the selected printer. If you marked a font with an asterisk (*), highlight it again and type another * to unmark it. If you marked the font with a plus (+), type + again to unmark it.

SEE ALSO

Base Font; Font; Printer, Select.

Case Conversion

Converts a marked block of text to uppercase or lowercase letters.

SEQUENCE OF STEPS

Alt-F4 (Block) *or* ⌐ **E**dit pull-down *then* **B**lock

➥ *[highlight text]*

➡ **Shift-F3** (Switch) *then* **U**ppercase; **L**owercase *or*
⌐ **E**dit pull-down *then* Con**v**ert Case *then* To
Upper; To **L**ower

USAGE

To convert a block of text to all uppercase or all lowercase
letters, simply mark it as a block with the Block option and
then select Switch (Shift-F3) or Convert Case (from the Edit
pull-down menu). To convert the marked text, select Uppercase or Lowercase.

Note that converting text to lowercase will not affect a
capital letter at the beginning of a sentence. For example,

...and John Smith. He...

becomes

...and john smith. He...

Center

Centers text on a line between the left and right margins.

SEQUENCE OF STEPS

To center text as you type it:

Shift-F6 (Center) *or* **L**ayout pull-down *then* **A**lign *then*
Center

➡ *<text to be centered>* ↵

To center existing text:

Alt-F4 (Block) *or* ⌐ **E**dit pull-down *then* **B**lock

➡ *[highlight text to be centered]*

➡ **Shift-F6** (Center) *or* ⌐ **L**ayout pull-down *then*
Align *then* **C**enter

➠ [Just:Center]? **No** (**Yes**)

USAGE

To center text on a line between the left and right margin settings, select Center, type the text, and press the Enter key. To center text after it has been entered, mark the text (this can include several lines) with Block, then select Center. WordPerfect will prompt you. To center marked text, select Yes.

To remove centering, locate either the [Center] or the [Just:Center] code in the Reveal Codes screen and delete it.

SEE ALSO

Block Operations; Flush Right; Center Page (Top to Bottom).

Center Page (Top to Bottom)

Centers text on a page between the top and bottom margins.

SEQUENCE OF STEPS

Ctrl-Home ↑

➠ **Shift-F8** (Format) *or* ⌨ **L**ayout pull-down

➠ **P**age

➠ **C**enter Page (top to bottom) **Y**

➠ **F7** (Exit)

USAGE

Use the Center Page (Top to Bottom) command to print less than an entire page of text centered vertically between your top and bottom margins, as in title sheets of reports and papers.

When using this command, position the cursor at the very top of the page before entering the [Center Pg] code.

To remove centering on the page, locate and delete the [Center Pg] code in the Reveal Codes screen.

SEE ALSO

Center.

Codes

Instructs the printer on how to format the text and graphics in your document.

SEQUENCE OF STEPS

Alt-F3 (Reveal Codes) *or* ⌐ **E**dit *then* **R**eveal Codes

➡ *[view or edit codes and text in the Reveal Codes screen]*

➡ **Alt-F3** (Reveal Codes) *or* ⌐ **E**dit *then* **R**eveal Codes

---

USAGE

WordPerfect enters formatting codes into your document as you use various commands. These codes are then sent to your printer when you print the document. They instruct the printer on how to accomplish various formatting changes in the document.

Some codes, like those used to boldface and underline text, are inserted in pairs, with one code turning on the effect and the other one turning it off.

WordPerfect keeps the formatting codes hidden from view on the editing screen. To see them, you must press Reveal Codes (Alt-F3), or select Reveal codes from the Edit pull-down menu. This causes the program to split the screen into two windows. The lower window shows the text with all of the codes inserted by WordPerfect commands. WordPerfect indicates the position of the cursor in the Reveal Codes screen by highlighting the code or character. When using Reveal Codes, you can use all of the standard WordPerfect editing features (including Undelete). When you want the Reveal Codes screen to disappear, select Reveal Codes a second time.

In WordPerfect 5.1, you can adjust the size of this window, which is normally 11 lines, by selecting Screen (Ctrl-F3) when the Reveal Codes window is displayed and choosing Window, then entering the number of lines you want it to have (the maximum screen size is 24 lines). If you are using pull-down menus, choose Edit and then Window.

Most of the time you use the Reveal Codes screen to locate the position of a code that you wish to delete or change (you can't always tell when the cursor is on a code just by looking at the regular editing screen). To quickly locate the position of a code, you can use WordPerfect's Search feature (see **Search: Searching for Format Codes**).

You can prevent a formatting change that you have introduced in the document by locating and deleting the code in the Reveal Codes screen. If the cursor is located on the code, press the Del key to remove it. If the cursor is after the code, press the Backspace key to remove it.

Columns, Text (Newspaper and Parallel)

Allows you to format your text using either newspaper or parallel columns.

SEQUENCE OF STEPS

To define newspaper or parallel text columns:

Alt-F7 (Columns/Tables) *or* ⌐⊟ **L**ayout pull-down

⤑ **C**olumns

⤑ **D**efine

➠ **T**ype; **N**umber of Columns; **D**istance Between Columns; **M**argins

➠ **F7** (Exit)

To turn text columns on and off in the document:

Alt-F7 (Columns/Tables) *or* ▭ **L**ayout pull-down

➠ **C**olumns

➠ **O**n; O**ff**

Note: If you are using WordPerfect 5.0, the Alt-F7 key is called Math/Columns. Column Define and Column On/Off are options on the menu that appears when you press Alt-F7.

USAGE	

WordPerfect can automatically format two different types of text columns: *newspaper* (also called "winding" or "snaking" columns) and *parallel* (or "comparison") columns. Neither of these is to be confused with tabular columns, which are set simply by pressing Tab to go the next tab stop. Newspaper columns are used with continuous text (as in a newsletter), for which it does not matter where the material in the column ends, because the program wraps the text to the top of the next column. Parallel columns are used when the material consists of separate items that should remain together on a page (as in scripts).

There are several basic steps involved in using either type of text column:

1. Position the cursor at the beginning of the area to be formatted in columns or anywhere before this point in the document;

2. Define the columns;

3. Turn on the columns;

4. Enter the text for the columns;

5. Turn off the columns.

WordPerfect 5.1's Tables feature can also be used for parallel columns (see **Tables**).

Defining the Columns

The steps involved in defining Newspaper and Parallel columns are very similar:

1. Select Columns/Tables (Alt-F7) or use the Layout pull-down menu.

2. Select Columns. (In version 5.0, select Column Def in place of steps 2 and 3.)

3. Select the Define option.

4. Select the Type option. WordPerfect displays the options

   Column Type: **1 N**ewspaper; **2 P**arallel; **3** Parallel with **B**lock Protect: **0**

5. Choose the appropriate column type.

6. Select the Number option and enter the number of columns you want (the default is 2 and you can set up to 24).

7. WordPerfect automatically calculates the distance between columns depending upon the number and the margin settings. To override this distance, select the Distance Between Columns option and enter the distance you want to use.

8. WordPerfect automatically calculates the left and right margin settings for the columns depending upon the number of columns, the distance between them, and the margin settings. If you wish to have unequal columns, select the Margins option and the the left and right margin settings for the column (or columns) you wish to change.

9. Press Exit (F7) to save your column definition.

When you define text columns, WordPerfect inserts a [Col Def: . . .] code in your document.

Turning On the Columns

After defining the columns, you are returned to the Columns menu. If you wish to use your columns at the cursor's present position, select the On option in version 5.1, or the Column On/Off option in version 5.0. If you wish to use the columns somewhere later on in the document, exit from this menu, move the cursor to the place where you want your columns to begin, and then return to this option. When you turn on columns, WordPerfect inserts the code [Col On] in the document.

You can't use the Column On/Off option on the Columns menu until after you have defined your columns. If you have defined several different columns in a document, WordPerfect will use the one whose [Col Def: . . .] code immediately precedes the [Col On] code.

Editing the Text Columns

When typing or editing the text for your columns, you can use most WordPerfect editing features. However, you can't sort, add footnotes, or change the margin settings. In addition, movement between columns is a little different in Column mode; these techniques are summarized in Table 2. The delete keys work within a single column. This means that pressing Delete to the End of Page (Ctrl-Page Down) deletes from the cursor to the end of the column. If you have an advanced keyboard, Alt-← and Alt-→ move from column to column.

You can use Move (Ctrl-F4) to cut or copy a sentence or paragraph in a single column. However, to cut or copy an entire column (equivalent to a page), you must use Block (Alt-F4) with Block Move or Copy. Do not try to use the Tabular Column option to move a column, as a text column is not defined by Tab stops and can't be properly retrieved as a tabular column.

Newspaper Columns

When entering text in newspaper-style columns, WordPerfect inserts a Soft Page code [SPg] when you reach the bottom margin of the page and the cursor moves to the top of the next column. To end a column before you reach the bottom margin, press Hard Page (Ctrl-Enter) to insert a Hard

KEY SEQUENCE	RESULT
Ctrl-Home → or ←	Moves cursor between columns
Ctrl-Home Home ←	Moves to the first column
Ctrl-Home Home →	Moves to the last column
→	Moves to the first character of the next column when the cursor is on the last character in one column
←	Moves to the last character of the previous column when the cursor is on the first character in one column
Ctrl-Return	Ends a column and moves to the next column; In a rightmost newspaper-style column, also creates a page break

Note: Other cursor control key sequences work as they do in Editing mode and scroll all columns simultaneously.

Table 2: Cursor Movement in Column Mode

Page code [HPg]. To shorten the length of all newspaper columns on the page, increase the bottom margin.

Parallel Columns

When entering text in parallel columns, press Hard Page (Ctrl-Enter) to move to the next column across. When you press Hard Page after entering the text for the last column, the cursor returns to the beginning of the first column. If you are using parallel columns without block protection, the codes

[Col Off]; [HRt]; [Col On]

are inserted into the document at this point. If you are using parallel columns with block protection, the codes

[BlockPro:Off][Col Off]; [Hrt]; [BlockPro:On][Col On]

are inserted into the document. All items between the [Block-
Pro:On] and [BlockPro:Off] codes are kept together on a page.
If the material will be split across pages by a soft page break
[SPg], WordPerfect will move it all to the next page.

Turning Off the Columns

When you are finished entering your columns and wish to
return to the normal format of your document, you need
to turn off the columns. To do this, press Columns/Tables
(Alt-F7), then select the Columns option, and select Off.
WordPerfect inserts a [Col Off] code in your document at the
cursor's position.

SEE ALSO

Tabs; Tables.

Compose

Allows you to create digraphs and diacriticals or select a
special symbol or character from one of WordPerfect's character sets.

SEQUENCE OF STEPS

To create a digraph or diacritical:

Ctrl-2 (Compose) *or* ⌐⊏⊐ **F**ont pull-down *then*
Characters

➠ *<first character><second character>*

To select a character from one of WordPerfect's character sets:

Ctrl-2 (Compose) *or* ⌐⊏⊐ **F**ont pull-down *then*
Characters

➠ *<character set number>,<character number>* ↵

USAGE ══════════════

You can use Compose (Ctrl-2) to create digraphs like æ or diacriticals like é or ñ. To produce such characters, press Compose (Ctrl-2) or choose Characters from the Font menu, and then enter the two characters that make up the special character. (The order in which the characters are entered doesn't matter.) If you type the **a** and **e**, for example, æ will appear at the cursor's position. However, the fact that you can create these special characters on your screen doesn't mean that your printer can reproduce them. This depends upon the printer and fonts that you are using.

You can also use Compose to produce specific characters in one of the many characters sets created by WordPerfect. Each set is assigned a number, as is each character in that set. To view the character sets, you need to retrieve the document CHARACTR.DOC on the Conversion disk. You can also retrieve the document CHARMAP.TST to see which of these characters your printer can produce.

To enter a character from one of these sets, first press Compose (Ctrl-2) or select characters from the Font pull-down menu. Enter the number of the character set, type a comma, and enter the number of the character in that set. Then press ↵. For example, to enter the 1/2 symbol, which is character 17 of character set 4, you press Compose (Ctrl-2), then enter **4,17** and press ↵. If your printer can't produce the character you entered with Compose, you will see a solid rectangle instead of the desired character in your document. If your printer can print graphics, WordPerfect 5.1 will create that character for it.

WordPerfect doesn't enter any codes when you type a special character with Compose. Therefore, to remove the character, simply delete it as you would any other character in the document.

SEE ALSO ══════════════

Overstrike.

Conditional End of Page

Ensures that a specific number of lines of text remain together on a page.

SEQUENCE OF STEPS

[move the cursor to the line above the lines to keep together]

➡ **Shift-F8** (Format) *or* ⌨ **L**ayout pull-down

➡ **O**ther

➡ **C**onditional End of Page

➡ *<number of lines>*↵

➡ **F7** (Exit)

USAGE

The Conditional End of Page command is used to keep a group of lines together on a page. Once the group of lines is marked, if subsequent changes to an earlier part of the document result in a soft page break within the block, WordPerfect will move the entire block to the beginning of the next page (resulting in a shorter previous page).

To use the Conditional End of Page command, you must first count the number of lines you want to keep together and locate the cursor somewhere on the line above the group. Then, follow the step sequence shown above. To remove the conditional end of page, locate the [Cndl EOP] code in the Reveal Codes screen and delete it.

NOTE

You can also use Block Protect to accomplish the same thing. When you use this command, you don't have to know the number of lines involved, as you indicate the text to stay on a page by marking it as a block.

SEE ALSO

Block Protect; Widow/Orphan Protection.

Copying Files

Allows you to copy files between disks and directories from within WordPerfect.

SEQUENCE OF STEPS

To copy a single file located in the current directory:

F5 (List Files) ↵ *or* ⌐ **F**ile pull-down *then* List **F**iles

➤ *[highlight file]*

➤ **C**opy

➤ Copy this file to: *<drive letter/path name>* ↵

To copy multiple files located in the current directory:

F5 (List Files) ↵

➤ *[type * before each file to be copied]*

➤ **C**opy

➤ Copy marked files? **N**o (**Y**es)

➤ Copy all marked files to: *<drive letter/path name>* ↵

USAGE

WordPerfect allows you to copy files to a new disk or directory from the List Files menu. To copy a single file, highlight the name on the List Files screen and select the Copy option. WordPerfect will display the prompt: *Copy this file to:*. Enter the drive letter (as in **B**:) if you want to copy the file to a new disk. Enter the entire path name (as in **C:\WP\LTRS**), if you want to copy it to a new directory.

To copy multiple files at one time, mark each file by high-lighting it and typing an asterisk (*). To copy all of the files in the list, press Alt-F5 and select the Copy option. When you are prompted, choose Yes. Designate the drive/directory for these copies in response to the prompt *Copy all marked files to:* and press ↵.

SEE ALSO

Directories: Changing Directories; List Files.

Cross-Reference (5.1) or Automatic Reference (5.0)

Allows you to mark references in the document to a figure, table, footnote, or page; automatically updates them.

SEQUENCE OF STEPS

To mark both the reference and target, (first move to the place where the reference is to appear):

Alt-F5 (Mark Text) *or* ⌐ **M**ark pull-down

➦ Cross-**R**ef

➦ Mark **B**oth Reference and Target

➦ **P**age Number; Paragraph/**O**utline Number; **F**ootnote Number; **E**ndnote Number; **G**raphics Box Number

➦ *[position cursor immediately after the target]* ↵

➦ *<target name>* ↵

To mark only the reference (first move to the place where the reference is to appear):

Alt-F5 (Mark Text) *or* ⌐ *M*ark pull-down

➦ Cross-**R**ef

➦ Mark **R**eference

➧ **P**age Number; Paragraph/**O**utline Number; **F**ootnote Number; **E**ndnote Number; **G**raphics Box Number

➧ *<target name>* ↵

To mark only the target (first position the cursor immediately after the target):

Alt-F5 (Mark Text) *or* ▭ **M**ark pull-down

➧ Cross-**R**ef

➧ Mark **T**arget

➧ *<target name>* ↵

To generate the cross-references (you will need to do this any time a reference is affected by editing the document):

Alt-F5 (Mark Text) *or* ▭ **M**ark pull-down

➧ **G**enerate

➧ **G**enerate Tables, Indexes, Cross-References, etc.

➧ Existing tables, lists, and indexes will be replaced. Continue? Yes (**No**) ↵

USAGE

The Cross-Reference feature, called Automatic Reference in version 5.0, maintains and automatically updates references to areas of text, footnotes, endnotes, graphics boxes, or equation boxes (version 5.1). The place in the document where the reference number will appear when the document is printed is the *reference*. The place in the document that contains the text referred to is the *target*.

You can mark the reference and target at the same time except when referencing a graphics box caption. In this case, you must mark the reference and the target separately. When you mark a reference only, a question mark appears in place of the reference number. This question mark is replaced with the actual figure, note, or page number when you generate the references.

SEE ALSO

Graphics; Mark Text; Master Document.

Cursor Movement

WordPerfect has many key combinations that move the cursor through a document, as shown inside the back cover of this book. However, you can only use these techniques to move through existing text or codes. WordPerfect will not allow you to move the cursor beyond the last text character or formatting code.

Using the Mouse to Position the Cursor

If you are using a mouse, simply click with the left mouse button at the point where you want to position the cursor. If you have split the screen, you can use the mouse in either window. You can also use it to position the cursor in prompts that ask for input from the keyboard.

If you need to see parts of your document that are not visible on the screen, you can use the mouse to scroll to them. Press the right mouse button and then drag the mouse to the edge of the screen in the direction you want to scroll (right, left, up, or down). To stop scrolling, release the mouse button. To block text and scroll at the same time, use the left mouse button.

You can also use the mouse to select WordPerfect commands and features (see **Mouse**).

SEE ALSO

Esc Key; Go To; Mouse.

Cut and Copy Text

Allows you to move or copy text within a document or between two documents.

SEQUENCE OF STEPS

To move or copy a sentence, paragraph, or page:

Ctrl-F4 (Move) *or* ꭚꭔ **E**dit pull-down *then* **S**elect

➥ **S**entence; **P**aragraph; **P**age

➥ **M**ove; **C**opy

➥ *[move cursor to place where text is to be moved or copied]* ↵

To move or copy a marked block, column, or rectangle:

➥ **Ctrl-F4** (Move) *or* ꭚꭔ **E**dit pull-down *then* **M**ove (Cut); **C**opy

➥ **B**lock; **T**abular **C**olumn; **R**ectangle

➥ **M**ove; **C**opy

➥ *[move cursor to place where text is to be moved or copied]* ↵

USAGE

WordPerfect provides two methods for moving (cutting) or copying text, with or without using a mouse (version 5.1). In addition, if you have an enhanced keyboard, version 5.1 provides keyboard shortcuts for these operations. When you move text, it is cut from its original position and relocated in the new position you indicate. When you copy text, it remains in its original position and is copied to the new position you indicate. To move or copy text between document windows, press Switch (Shift-F3) before pressing ⏎ to retrieve the text. To be able to press ⏎ without inserting the copied or moved text, press F1 (Cancel); then to retrieve the text where you want it, press Shift-F10 ⏎.

If you want to move or copy a tabular column (see **Marking a Tabular Column**), a rectangle (see **Marking a Rectangle**), or any block that is not an entire sentence, paragraph, or page, you need to mark the block before you move or copy it.

Text that has been moved or copied remains in a special place in the computer's memory (known as a *buffer*) even after it has been retrieved the first time. To retrieve another copy of the text elsewhere in the document, take these steps:

1. Relocate the cursor to the place where you want the second copy to appear.

2. Press Move (Ctrl-F4). If you are using pull-down menus, select Paste from the Edit menu.

3. Select Retrieve.

4. Select the appropriate option: Block (use this option even if you cut or copied an entire sentence, paragraph, or page); Tabular Column; or Rectangle.

You can also retrieve text by pressing Retrieve (Shift-F10) and then the ⏎ key.

With WordPerfect 5.1, you can use keyboard shortcuts for moving and copying text on some keyboards. Block the text; then press Ctrl-Del to move it or Ctrl-Ins to copy it.

Marking a Tabular Column

To mark a tabular column for moving or copying, you must separate each column by at least one tab stop. Move the cursor to the first tab stop in the first line of the column. Press Block, then move the cursor to the beginning of the column in the last line. Then press Move and select the Tabular Column option. WordPerfect will highlight just the column. With a mouse, highlight to the end of the column (more will be highlighted than you want, but don't worry); then choose Select from the Edit menu. Tabular Column will be selected for you, so just press ↵. Finally, choose either Copy or Move and complete the procedure by moving the cursor to the column's new position and pressing ↵.

Marking a Rectangle

A rectangular block is marked for moving or copying from corner to corner. To mark a rectangle, position the cursor at one corner—either the upper left or the lower right—and press Block. Then move the cursor to the opposite corner and press Move. (A regular text block will be highlighted until you choose Rectangle.) Select Rectangle, choose either Copy or Move, and complete the procedure by moving the cursor to the rectangle's new position and pressing ↵. You can also use the mouse to highlight the block.

To abandon the move or copy operation that you have initiated, press Cancel (F1). If the marked block disappears from your editing screen when you use Cancel, press Move (Ctrl-F4) and select the Retrieve and Block (or Column or Rectangle) options to have it reappear in its original position.

SEE ALSO

Append Block; Deleting Text: Deleting a Block.

Date, Inserting the

Inserts the current date either as text or as a function that is updated when the document is retrieved or printed.

SEQUENCE OF STEPS

To enter the date text or Date code in the document:

Shift-F5 (Date/Outline) *or* ▭ **T**ools pull-down

➠ Date **T**ext; Date **C**ode

To change the date format:

Shift-F5 (Date/Outline) *or* ▭ **T**ools pull-down

➠ Date **F**ormat

➠ *<date format codes>* ⏎

➠ **F7** (Exit)

USAGE

You can use the Date Text and Date Code options to insert the current date and/or time in your document. If you select the Date Text option, the date is entered as text and doesn't change. If you select Date Code, the date is entered as a function code that is updated whenever you retrieve or print the document. You can format the date in a variety of ways by using the Date Format option.

To insert the current date or time during a merge, use the {DATE} merge code (see **Merge Operations: Merge Codes**).

To remove the date inserted as text, delete it as you would any text in WordPerfect. To remove the Date code, locate and delete the [Date] code in the Reveal Codes screen.

SEE ALSO

Merge Operations: Merge Codes.

Decimal/Align Character

Allows you to enter a new character for the decimal point (and tab alignment character) and thousands' separator.

SEQUENCE OF STEPS

Shift-F8 (Format) *or* ⌐⍐ **L**ayout pull-down

➤ **O**ther

➤ **D**ecimal/Align Character *<character>* ⏎ Thousands' Separator *<character>* ⏎

➤ **F7** (Exit)

USAGE

WordPerfect uses the period as the decimal and alignment character and the comma as the thousands' separator. To change these, follow the key sequence shown above. A change to the decimal/align character affects how Tab Align and totals calculated with the Math feature work.

SEE ALSO

Math; Tab Align.

Deleting Files

Allows you to delete files from within WordPerfect without having to exit to DOS.

SEQUENCE OF STEPS

To delete a single file in the current directory:

F5 (List Files) ↵ *or* ⌐ᗺ **F**ile pull-down *then* List **F**iles

➠ *[highlight file name]*

➠ **D**elete

➠ Delete *<file name>*? **N**o (**Y**es)

To delete several files in the current directory at one time:

F5 (List Files) ↵ *or* ⌐ᗺ **F**ile pull-down *then* List **F**iles

➠ *[Enter * before each file to be deleted]*

➠ **D**elete

➠ Delete marked files? **N**o (**Y**es)

USAGE

By using the Delete option on the List Files menu, you can delete unneeded document files from within WordPerfect without having to use the DOS delete commands.

To delete a document from the List Files menu, press F5 (or choose List Files from the File pull-down menu) and enter a new drive/directory if the files aren't in the current directory; otherwise, just press ↵. Move the highlight cursor to the file to be deleted. If you want to delete several files, mark each one by typing an asterisk (*) by its name. In Word-Perfect 5.1, you can mark all the files in a directory with an asterisk by pressing Mark Text (Alt-F5); pressing Alt-F5 a second time will unmark all of the files. Then select the Delete option and confirm the deletion by selecting Yes.

You can't restore a deleted file in WordPerfect as you can deleted text. Therefore, use the Delete option on List Files with care. If you do delete a file in error, turn to DOS utilities like Norton Utilities or Mace Utilities to restore the file.

SEE ALSO

Directories: Changing Directories.

Deleting Text

Allows you to delete any amount of text in the document.

SEQUENCE OF STEPS

See Table 3.

USAGE

WordPerfect includes a wide variety of methods for deleting text in the document. All methods are summarized in Table 3.

To restore the text you just deleted, press Cancel (F1) and select the Restore option. With pull-down menus, select Undelete from the Edit menu.

SEE ALSO

Codes; Undelete.

TO DELETE	PRESS
Character by character	Backspace (deletes to left of cursor); Del (deletes character or space the cursor is on)
Word by word	Ctrl-Backspace
Several words	Esc *n* (*n* = number of words to left of the cursor) Ctrl-Backspace
The word to the left of the cursor	Ctrl-← Ctrl-Backspace
The word to the right of the cursor	Ctrl-→ Ctrl-Backspace

Table 3: Methods for Deleting Text in WordPerfect

TO DELETE	PRESS
From the cursor left to the beginning of a word	Home Backspace
From the cursor right to the end of a word	Home Del
To the end of a line	Ctrl-End
To the end of a page	Ctrl-PgDn
A sentence	Ctrl-F4 S D or Edit *then* Select *then* Sentence *then* Delete
A paragraph	Ctrl-F4 P D or Edit *then* Select *then* Paragraph *then* Delete
A page	Ctrl-F4 A D or Edit *then* Select *then* Page *then* Delete
A marked block	Backspace Y or Del Y or Edit *then* Delete *then* Yes

Table 3: Methods for Deleting Text in WordPerfect (continued)

Directories

Allows you to create and delete directories from within WordPerfect and to change the current (or default) directory.

SEQUENCE OF STEPS

To create a new directory:

F5 (List Files) *or* ⌨ **F**ile pull-down *then* List **F**iles

➠ **=** *or* ⏎ *then* **O**ther Directory

➠ *<drive/directory path name>* ⏎

➠ Create *<drive/directory path name>*? **N**o (**Y**es)

To make an existing directory current (the default):

F5 (List Files) *or* ⌨ **F**ile pull-down *then* List **F**iles⏎

➠ **=** *or* ⏎ *then* **O**ther Directory

➠ New directory = *<drive/directory path name>* ⏎

➠ Cancel (**F1**) to return to screen

To delete a directory (after removing all its files):

F5 (List Files) ⏎ *or* ⌨ **F**ile pull-down *then* List **F**iles

➠ *[highlight directory name]*

➠ **D**elete

➠ Delete *<drive/directory path name>*? **N**o (**Y**es)

To give a directory a descriptive alias:

[enter existing directory pathname] **F9** (End Field)

➠ **F9** *<descriptive alias>* **F9** (End Field)

➠ **Shift-F9** (Merge Codes)

➠ End Record

➠ **=** **F10** (Save) \wp{wp}.dln ⏎

USAGE

WordPerfect allows you to manage your document files by saving them in different directories. Usually the directories that contain your documents are organized as subdirectories of the WordPerfect directory (such as C:\WP\FILES) that contains the WordPerfect program files. You can create and remove such directories from within WordPerfect instead of resorting to the DOS Make Directory (md) command. However, WordPerfect won't let you delete any directory until you have removed all of the files within it (see **Deleting Files**).

Creating Directories

To create a new directory, perform the procedure to change directories (outlined in the step sequence above). When WordPerfect finds that the directory doesn't exist, it prompts you to create it. If you type **Y** for Yes, the program creates the directory for you.

Path Names

When entering the path name for the directory, begin with the drive letter and a colon (such as **B:**, **C:**, or **D:**) if it is on another drive and then list all of the directories in the hierarchy, separated by the back slash (\). If the directory is on the same disk, you need only enter the directory names separated by back slashes.

Using Directory Aliases

In versions of WordPerfect prior to 5.1, you were restricted to the DOS naming conventions (eight characters plus an optional three-character extension) when naming directories. In WordPerfect 5.1, you can give a directory a more descriptive name of up to 30 characters, called an alias. The alias will be displayed when you have the Long Display option on in the List Files screen (see **List Files**).

To create a directory alias, in a blank editing screen type the full DOS path name of the existing directory. Then press F9 and type the descriptive alias name. Press Shift-F9 (Merge Codes) and select End Record. An example on your screen should look like this:

C:\Wp51\lotus{END FIELD}

October spreadsheets{END FIELD}

{END RECORD}

From then on, the directory named LOTUS will appear as OCTOBER SPREADSHEETS when you display the List Files screen and the Long Display option is on.

You can give any of your existing directories aliases by repeating this procedure for each of them. When you have finished assigning aliases, save the file as **wp{wp}.dln** in your root directory (C:). Whenever you want to assign aliases to other directories, retrieve this file, edit it to assign the new aliases, and save it.

Changing Directories

You can change the current (or default) directory in Word-Perfect using List Files (F5) from either the editing screen or the List Files menu. To change the directory from the editing screen, press List Files (F5) (or select List Files from the File pull-down menu) and type =. Then enter the new drive/directory path in response to the *New directory* = prompt and press ⏎. Edit the current path name displayed after this prompt or retype it from scratch.

WordPerfect responds by showing you the new default directory, terminated by *.* (the global wild cards for listing all files in the directory). To return to the editing screen, press Cancel (F1). To obtain a listing of all of the files in the new default directory, press ⏎.

Finding and Changing the Current Directory

If you don't know the name of the default directory or where it is located on the path, you can change the directory using the Other Directory option on the List Files menu. To view aliases you have assigned if the List Files screen is not showing the long display, select the Short/Long Display option and choose Long Display. If the name of the desired directory appears at the top of the list, move the highlight cursor to it. If it is located on a level above that of the current directory, highlight .. *Parent <Dir>* and press ⏎ twice. Then locate and highlight the directory name on the new list. If the desired directory is a subdirectory of one shown on the list, highlight that directory and press ⏎ twice (or double-click on the directory and press ⏎ or the right mouse button), then move the highlight cursor to its name on the new list. Select the Other Directory option, and WordPerfect will supply the path to the highlighted directory as the new directory to change to; to accept it press ↵. To return to the editing screen, press Cancel (F1) twice. To obtain a directory listing of all of the files in the new default directory, press ↵.

Deleting Directories

To delete a directory, first make sure that there are no files in it. You can do this by changing to the directory and listing the files as outlined above. With the highlight cursor on the directory name, select the Delete option on the List Files menu (F5 ↵) and answer Yes to the prompt to delete the directory.

SEE ALSO

Deleting Files; List Files; Short/Long Document Names.

Display Pitch

Adjusts the amount of space that one character occupies on the display screen.

SEQUENCE OF STEPS

Shift-F8 (Format) *or* ⌨ **L**ayout

➠ **D**ocument

➠ **D**isplay Pitch Automatic **Y** *or* **N** *<width>* ↵

➠ **F7** (Exit)

USAGE

WordPerfect displays all characters on the screen in a mono-spaced pitch of 10 characters per inch, regardless of what font you are using. Sometimes, when you're setting up complex tables or using the Advance feature, some characters will overlap and therefore not be visible on the screen. To help you see the spacing between characters, you can change the display pitch on the Document menu, accessed from Format (Shift-F8).

There are two options attached to Display Pitch: Automatic, which is set to Yes or No, and Width, which allows you to enter a measurement for increasing or decreasing the display pitch. When Automatic is set to Yes, you cannot change the display pitch. If you set Automatic to No, you can change it from the default setting of 0.1".

You can change the display pitch from anywhere in the document; the new pitch affects the entire document. To return the document to the normal display width of one-tenth inch, return to the Display Pitch option and enter **Y** for the Auto setting and **.1** as the Width measurement.

Document Comments

Places nonprinting comments in your document.

SEQUENCE OF STEPS

To create or edit a comment or convert a comment to text:

Ctrl-F5 (Text In/Out) *then* **C**omment *or* ⌐▲ **E**dit
  pull-down *then* **C**omment

➠ **C**reate; **E**dit; Convert to **T**ext

To convert text to a comment:

Alt-F4 (Block)

➠ *[highlight text to be placed in comment]*

➡ **Ctrl-F5** (Text In/Out) *or* ▭ **E**dit pull-down *then* **C**omment *then* **C**reate

➡ Create a comment? **No** (**Y**es)

USAGE

WordPerfect allows you to enter nonprinting comments anywhere in the text of your document. These comments can be used as reminders of editing changes that still remain to be done. You can use the Search feature to quickly locate comments in the text because WordPerfect inserts the code [Comment] in the document when you create a comment (see **Search: Searching for Format Codes**).

On the editing screen, the text entered as a comment is displayed within a double-lined box. If you create the comment in the middle of a line, the comment box will split the sentence on different lines, although the cursor will bypass the comment box when moving from the part of the sentence before the comment to the part after it.

WordPerfect allows you to convert the text entered into a comment box into document text, which will be printed. To do this, you follow the procedure for editing a comment except that you select the Convert to Text option on the Comment menu. The box surrounding the comment disappears, and WordPerfect reformats the text as required.

You can also convert document text to comment text, so that it is no longer part of the document, nor is it printed. First, block the text to be converted, then select Edit and Comment. When you do this, a prompt will appear. When you select Yes, the text will be enclosed in a comment box.

To remove a comment from the document, locate and delete the [Comment] code in the Reveal Codes screen.

SEE ALSO

Document Summary.

Document Compare

Compares the copy of your document on the editing screen with the disk version and marks the differences.

SEQUENCE OF STEPS

To compare a document on screen with a document on disk:

Alt-F5 (Mark Text) *or* ⌨ **M**ark pull-down

➠ **G**enerate

➠ **C**ompare Screen and Disk Document and Add Redline and Strikeout

➠ **O**ther Document: *<file name>* ↵

To remove all redline markings and strikeout text added when using Document Compare:

Alt-F5 (Mark Text) *or* ⌨ **M**ark pull-down

➠ **G**enerate

➠ **R**emove Redline Markings and Strikeout Text from Document

➠ Delete redline markings and strikeout text? **No** (**Yes**)

Note: You can also choose Document Compare from the Mark pull-down menu; then choose Add Markings or Remove Markings.

USAGE

This feature checks the document on the editing screen against any version of the document on disk. It compares only phrases in the two documents and automatically indicates any discrepancies between the two by marking the document on your screen. WordPerfect considers a phrase to be any text between markers, including any punctuation marks, hard returns, hard page breaks, Footnote and Endnote codes, and the end of the document.

If phrases that don't exist in the disk version have been added to the document on screen, WordPerfect redlines the text in the screen version. If phrases that still exist in the disk version no longer exist in the document on screen, the program marks the text with strikeout. If phrases have been moved in the document on screen from their position in the disk version, WordPerfect inserts *THE FOLLOWING TEXT WAS MOVED* on a line before the text and *THE PRECEDING TEXT WAS MOVED* on a line after the text. These messages are displayed in strikeout, and the text in between them may be displayed in either redline or strikeout, depending on the version in which it exists.

After running the Document Compare procedure as outlined by the key sequence above, you can locate the Redline codes and strikeout text by using the Search feature (see **Search: Searching for Format Codes**). After examining the changes, you can remove all Redline and Strikeout codes as indicated in the step sequence above.

SEE ALSO

Redline/Strikeout.

Document Summary

Enables you to add a nonprinting summary to your document.

SEQUENCE OF STEPS

To create or edit a document summary:

Shift-F8 (Format) *or* ⌨ Layout pull-down

➠ **D**ocument

➠ **S**ummary

➠ Creation **D**ate

➟ Document **N**ame

➟ Document Type: Au**t**hor/Typist; **S**ubject; **A**ccount; **K**eywords; **A**bstract

➟ **F7** (Exit)

To create a document summary on Save/Exit or set document summary defaults:

Shift-F1 (Setup) *or* ⌐⧵ File pull-down *then* **S**etup

➟ **E**nvironment

➟ **D**ocument Management/Summary

➟ **C**reate Summary on Save/Exit **N**o (**Y**es); **S**ubject Search Text; **L**ong Document Names **N**o (**Y**es); Default Document **T**ype

➟ **F7** (Exit)

Note: Several new options for the document summary feature were added to version 5.1. If you are using version 5.0, after you choose Document and then Summary, your choices will be **D**escriptive Filename; **S**ubject/**A**ccount; **A**uthor; **T**ypist; and **C**omments.

USAGE

You can add a document summary to any document that you create in WordPerfect. The document summary can be added or edited from any place within the document.

A document summary does not produce a code in your document, and with versions of WordPerfect prior to 5.1, there was no way to delete a document summary once it was created. With version 5.1, you can delete a document summary by pressing Del and typing **Y** in response to the prompt when the cursor is on the status line in the Document Summary menu.

The document summary can include the following statistics on the document (note that WordPerfect enters the first two automatically and you enter the rest):

• The date the document was created (WordPerfect uses the current date as supplied by DOS). You can change this date by using the Creation Date option. In addition, the summary displays the date of the latest revision.

- The long document name (see **Short/Long Document Names**), which can contain up to 68 characters, and a document type, which can be up to 20 characters (see below). If you have already assigned this document a long document name using List Files (see **List Files**), it will be displayed here, where you can edit it with the Document Name option.

- The author and/or typist, which can include up to 60 characters.

- The subject, which you can type in (up to 160 characters) or retrieve from a RE: heading in your document (see below).

- The account, which can be a number or any other information that will help you categorize the document.

- Any keywords that you want to use to identify the document. In List Files, you can use those keywords to help you locate the file or group of related files with the same keyword (see **List Files**).

- An abstract, which can be up to 780 characters. You can type in a summary of the document here, or press Retrieve (Shift-F10) to retrieve its first 400 characters.

Three items can be automatically retrieved from other locations in your document. When the cursor is on the status line in the Document Summary screen, you can press Shift-F10 (Retrieve) to retrieve (1) the most recent author and typist entries you have saved on any other document's document summary during your current session with Word-Perfect, (2) the first 39 characters following the first RE: in your document (you can change this search string; see below), and (3) the document's first 400 characters, which will appear as the Abstract entry. All three of these items will be located and retrieved if they exist; you can't choose a combination of them.

Setting Default Document Summary Options

The Document Management/Summary options on the Setup menu allow you to set defaults to use with your document summaries. You can have WordPerfect automatically prompt you to create a summary the first time you save each document by setting the Create Summary on Save/Exit option to Yes. The characters RE: are the default Subject Search Text, but you can change them to another subject heading, such as SUBJECT:, by using the Subject Search Text option. You can also specify with the Long Document Names option whether you want to use a long document name (up to 30 characters, including spaces) when you save each document. If you set this option to Yes, WordPerfect will prompt you to enter the long document name, the document type (see below), and the DOS file name for the document each time you save it. The Default Document Type option allows you to enter text that will be suggested as the Document Type when you save the document, assuming you are using long document names. In addition WordPerfect will suggest the first three characters of this document type as an extension when you save the document, so you can use this option to group related documents together, such as memos, letters, or chapters of different books.

Saving, Appending, and Printing Document Summaries

You can save a document summary as a separate file, or append it to an existing file. When the Document Summary menu is on the screen and the cursor is on the status line, press Save (F10) and enter a new or existing file name. If the file has already been created, you will be asked whether to replace its contents with the text of the document summary or append it to the end of the file.

To print a document summary, press Shift-F7 (Print) while the summary is displayed on your screen. In addition, if you are printing selected pages of a document (see **Printing**), you can type **s** to print the document summary.

If you are using the Look option in the List Files screen (F5), you can also save and print document summaries from there (*see* **List Files: Looking at the Contents of Files and Directories**).

Locating a File Using Its Document Summary Statistics

When you use the Look option on the List Files menu (F5 ↵) to view the contents of a document that contains a document summary, the summary statistics are always the first text displayed on the screen. You can also use the Find option (called Word Search in version 5.0) on the List Files menu to locate a file according to particular statistics in the document summary.

If you want to restrict the search to one specific word or word pattern that is in your document summaries, use the Document Summary option (see **Find** for the types of patterns you can enter). Use the First Pg option to search just the first pages (or the first 4000 characters, whichever occurs first) of each document. To search the entire document, select Entire Doc. Select Conditions to limit the search to a specific item within your document summaries, such as the author of the document or its date of creation. (See **Find**.)

SEE ALSO

Find; List Files: Looking at the Contents of Files and Directories.

Equations (Version 5.1)

In version 5.1, you can create mathematical equations.

| SEQUENCE OF STEPS |

To create an equation:

Alt-F9 (Graphics) *or* ⌐ **G**raphics pull-down

➠ **E**quation

➠ **C**reate

➠ **E**dit

➠ *[compose equation by typing or choosing from equation palette]*

➠ **F7 F7**(Exit)

To edit an existing equation in your document:

Alt-F9 (Graphics) *or* ⌐ **G**raphics pull-down

➠ **E**quation

➠ **E**dit

➠ *[enter equation number]*

To retrieve an existing equation file for editing:

Alt-F9 (Graphics) *or* ⌐ **G**raphics pull-down

➠ **E**quation

➠ **C**reate

➠ **E**dit

➠ **Shift-F10** (Retrieve) *[enter file name]* ↵ *or* **F5** *[enter directory name to view files]* ↵ *[highlight file]* **R**etrieve

To save an equation as a separate file (while you are in the equation editor:

Shift-F10 (Save) *[enter file name for equation]* ↵

| USAGE |

To create an equation, first define a graphics box as an equation box and then use the WordPerfect 5.1 equation editor to create your equation. As you enter the commands and keywords for your equation in the lower part of the window, the equation editor displays it graphically in the upper window so that you can see it as you compose it.

To create an equation, follow these steps:

1. Press Alt-F9 (Graphics), or select Equation from the Graphics menu.

2. Select Equation.

3. Select Create.

4. Select Edit to display the equation editor.

5. Create your equation in any combination of the following ways:

   • By typing in the equation editing window (the lower part of the screen). You can enter numbers, letters, and symbols from the keyboard. Certain keys have special meanings in the equation editor, and Word-Perfect recognizes many keywords as commands (see the Equation Palette appendix in your user guide for a complete list of these). You can also compose characters by using the Compose feature (see **Compose**).

   • By pressing F5 (List) or choosing List Commands to move to the equation palette (a series of menus similar to those found in the macro editor) and choosing symbols, commands, and variables from the items it presents. Select items with the mouse or the highlight cursor and then press ↵. After each selection you are moved back to the equation editing window.

6. Press Ctrl-F3 (Screen) or choose Screen Redisplay to view your equation in the display window (the upper part of the screen). To return to the equation editing window, press Shift-F3 or choose Screen Redisplay again.

7. Press F7 (Exit) to return to the equation definition screen.

In the equation editing window, you can delete characters by using the Backspace and Del keys. To delete from the

cursor to the end of the equation, press Ctrl-PgDn and respond **Yes** to the *Delete Remainder of Page?* prompt.

The equation you see in the equation display window is
normally larger than it will appear when printed (the percentage of magnification appears in the lower-right corner).
You can move and resize the equation, in the display window only, by using the arrow, PgUp, and PgDn keys. By
resizing you can check small symbols that may be used as
superscripts and subscripts, for example. Press Ctrl-Home
(Go To) to reset any changes you make to the display. You
can also move the equation around with the arrow keys, use
PgUp/PgDn Scale to resize the equation, and use **GoTo** Reset
to reset the equation display from the menu at the bottom of
the screen, when you switch to the display window.

When you are in the display window, a double line appears at its right, and you cannot use the cursor in the editing window. When you return to the editing window, the
double line moves to its right.

Saving an Equation as a Separate File

You can save an equation separately from the document it
appears in. You may want to do this, for example, if you plan
to use an equation in several documents. To save an equation, press F10 (Save) while you are in the equation editor;
then enter a name (a path name if you want to save it in a
different directory) and press ↵.

To retrieve a saved equation, press Shift-F10 (Retrieve)
while you are in the equation editor; then enter the name of
the equation. You can also press F5 (List Files) and enter a
directory name to display the files in a directory. Pressing F5
twice will display the contents of the current directory. In addition, you can enter an equation's name at the Filename
heading on the Definition: Equation menu, and WordPerfect
will retrieve the equation.

Printing Equations

Equations are printed in the base font you have selected unless you change the font within the equation box. You can also change the size (Small, Large, and so on) and appearance (bold, italic, and so on) of the font within the equation box. Variables (alphabetic characters) will automatically be printed in italics. Subscripts and superscripts will automatically be printed as subscripts and superscripts.

The program creates all equation symbols graphically. If you don't have a printer that will print graphics, set the Print as Graphics option on the Setup: Initial Settings menu to No. In this case WordPerfect will attempt to substitute a character in a different font for the symbol it needs to create; it will print a blank space if it cannot make a substitution.

To position the equation on the page, you position the graphics box that contains it (see **Graphics**). Although you can create equations in any type of graphics box, if you use an equation box, WordPerfect will automatically center it between the left and right margins, as is standard mathematical practice.

SEE ALSO

Graphics; Printing.

Esc Key

Repeats a character (other than a number) or cursor movement key pressed a specified number of times.

SEQUENCE OF STEPS

To repeat a character or cursor movement for the default repeat value:

Esc *<character or cursor movement key>*

To repeat a character or cursor movement for a new repeat value:

Esc *<number of times to repeat> <character or cursor movement key>*

USAGE

The Esc(ape) key in WordPerfect is used primarily to repeat a keyboard character (other than a number) or a cursor movement command. It is only secondarily used to cancel the current WordPerfect command (see **Canceling a Command**). When you press the Esc key, WordPerfect displays the prompt

Repeat Value = 8

If the next key you press is not a number, WordPerfect will enter that character eight times. If you press a cursor movement key, WordPerfect will repeat the cursor movement eight times.

If you press the Del(ete) key after pressing Esc, WordPerfect will delete the next eight characters from the cursor's position to the right. If you press the space bar after the Esc key, it will insert eight spaces.

You can vary the number of repetitions by entering a new repeat number before pressing the key. WordPerfect uses the new repeat value only that time and then returns to the default number.

SEE ALSO

Canceling a Command; List Files: Looking at the Contents of Files and Directories.

Exit

Quits WordPerfect and returns to DOS or clears the document editing screen to begin a new document.

F7 (Exit) *or* ⌦ **F**ile pull-down *then* **E**xit

➡ Save document? **Y**es (**N**o)

➡ Document to be saved: *<file name>* ⏎ Replace *<file name>* **N**o (**Y**es)

➡ Exit WordPerfect? **N**o (**Y**es)

USAGE

Exit (F7) is used to clear the current editing screen when you want to begin a new document, or to quit WordPerfect when you are finished using the word processor. You also use Exit to leave menus such as Setup, Format, and so on, and after entering the text of headers, footers, footnotes, and endnotes.

Saving and Exiting

When you press Exit during normal document editing, you see the prompt

Save document? **Y**es (**N**o)

Press ⏎ to accept the default setting of Yes, unless you wish to abandon the document and any editing you have made to it (thereby exiting without saving the document). When you press ⏎, WordPerfect will prompt you for the name of the document. Enter the document name if you haven't saved it before (see **Save**) and press ⏎. If you have already saved the document at least once, the prompt will contain the document name. If you want to save the document under a new name, type it in or edit the existing name. If you want to save it under the same name, simply press ⏎. WordPerfect will respond with the prompt

Replace *<file name>*? **N**o (**Y**es)

Choose Yes. After the document is saved, WordPerfect will prompt you either to exit the current document editing screen (if you are using both Doc 1 and Doc 2) or to exit

WordPerfect. The default response is No, so that you can press ↵ to remain in the current editing screen. If you decide not to clear your document from the editing screen, press Cancel (F1) to retain it and return to editing its text.

If you answer Yes to exiting WordPerfect, you will be returned to DOS or to the WordPerfect Library shell, if you use that utility. If you answer Yes to exiting the current document editing screen (either Doc 1 or Doc 2), you will be returned to the other editing screen. If you answer No to exiting WordPerfect or the current document editing screen, you will remain in it, and you can begin creating a new document (using the WordPerfect formatting defaults) or retrieve another document for editing.

If you are using long document names (see **Short/Long Document Names**), you will be prompted for a long document name as well as a document type when you exit. You can enter up to 68 characters, including spaces, for the name and up to 20 characters for the type, or, if the document has been previously saved, you can save it under the same name by pressing ↵ and choosing **Y** when you are prompted to confirm the replacement. WordPerfect will then show you the DOS file name, either its eight-character abbreviation of your long name (with an extension consisting of the first three letters of the document type) or a file name you used when saving the document previously.

Quitting WordPerfect without Using Exit

In WordPerfect it is important that you exit the program properly before you turn off the computer. WordPerfect automatically keeps special files, referred to as *overflow files*, that are not emptied and closed until you press F7 (Exit).

If you simply use Save (F10), and then turn off the power, WordPerfect will detect the presence of these files the next time you start the program and will beep and display this prompt on the initial startup screen:

Are other copies of WordPerfect currently running?
Yes (**N**o)

Responding No tells WordPerfect to erase the contents of the overflow files and move on to the standard editing screen.

SEE ALSO

Go To DOS/Shell; Save; Short/Long Document Names.

Find (5.1) *or* **Word Search (5.0)**

Locates all of the files in the current directory that contain a specified word or phrase.

SEQUENCE OF STEPS

To perform a word search in version 5.1:

F5 (List Files) ↵ *or* ⌐⊾ File pull-down *then* List Files ↵

➠ **Find**

➠ **N**ame; **D**oc Summary; First **P**g; **E**ntire Doc; **C**onditions; **U**ndo

➠ Word Pattern: *<word(s) or phrase>*

To set the search conditions in version 5.1:

F5 (List Files) ↵ *or* ⌐⊾ File pull-down *then* List Files ↵

➠ **Find**

➠ **C**onditions

➠ **P**erform Search; **R**eset Conditions; Revision **D**ate; **T**ext; Document **S**ummary (Creation Date; Document Name; Document Type; Author; Typist; Subject; Account; Keywords; Abstract)

➠ **F7** (Exit)

Note: In WordPerfect 5.0, Find is called Word Search, and the First Pg, Entire Doc, and Undo options appear on the Conditions submenu.

USAGE

The Find option of the List Files menu (called Word Search in WordPerfect 5.0) allows you to search through all the files in one directory or through the files you have explicitly marked with an asterisk (*) to find a specific word or phrase (up to 39 characters in 5.1 or 20 characters in 5.0).

Version 5.1   After WordPerfect locates the files that contain what you are searching for, it displays them separately. You can use the cursor keys to move among them, pressing ↵ to view their contents and determine which of them are the documents you are seeking. While you are looking at the contents of a file, you can use the Search feature (F2) to locate a particular word or phrase. You can also retrieve a marked file to the editing screen.

Version 5.0   After WordPerfect locates the files that contain what you are searching for, it marks them with an asterisk on the List Files screen. You can use the Look option to view their contents and determine which of them are the documents you are seeking. You can also retrieve a marked file to the editing screen.

Both Versions   To return to the List Files screen with the marked files still displayed, press Exit (F7). To return to List Files with the marked files displayed after retrieving a file, press List Files (F5) twice.

Setting Search Options

Version 5.1   Select Name from the Find menu to search for a file by name. You can enter part of a name pattern, and WordPerfect will display all the names of the files it finds that match that pattern (see **Entering Patterns** below).

The next three options on the Find menu allow you to specify which part of the document you want to search. Select Document Summary to search only in the document summaries of the files you have marked or of all the files in the directory, if you haven't marked any particular ones.

Select First Pg to search through only the first page or the first 4000 characters of each file.

Select Entire Document to search through all the files you have marked or all the files in the directory.

Select Conditions to enter specialized search conditions, as discussed below.

To repeat a search on the same group of files, select Undo. Normally, if you were searching through ten files and Word-Perfect located what you were searching for in two files, the next search you carried out would be on the two files that it located. Selecting this option brings you back to your original List Files screen—containing, in this example, ten files.

Version 5.0   After you select Word Search, you will see the following menu:

1 Document Summary; **2 F**irst Page; **3 E**ntire Document; **4 C**onditions:0

Select Document Summary for a word, phrase, or pattern only in the document summaries of the files you have marked or of all the files in the directory, if you haven't marked any particular ones.

Select First Page to search through only the first page or the first 4000 characters of each file.

Select Entire Document to search through all the files you have marked or all the files in the directory.

Select Conditions to enter specialized search conditions, as discussed below.

Setting Search Conditions

If you select Conditions, you can then choose the conditions that the files must meet.

The Perform Search On option lists the number of files that will be searched. After the search has finished, this number changes to the number of files that the search located. To start a search after selecting other search conditions, select this option.

Use the Reset Search Conditions option to clear the search conditions and enter new ones for the next search.

Revision Date allows you to specify that files created on or between certain dates be included in the search. You can enter the date with or without leading zeroes—as **01/02/91** or as **1/2/91**, for example.

Text allows you to combine three types of searches—document summaries, first page, and complete document—into one. You can enter a different search pattern for each and then search for all three patterns at once. When you have entered your patterns, select Perform Search to begin the search.

Document Summary allows you to search for specific items within your document summaries (see **Document Summary** for details about each of these items).

Version 5.0   The First Pg, Entire Doc, and Undo options, discussed under **Setting Search Options (version 5.1),** appear on this menu instead.

Entering Patterns for Word Searches

Both Versions: When you search a directory for a file containing a specific word or phrase that contains spaces, you must enter the word or phrase to be searched for in quotation marks.

You can search for an exact phrase by adding a blank space after the last letter and before the last quotation mark. You can also enter an exact phrase to be searched for by pressing Ctrl- ↵ before typing the phrase.

You can also use the wild cards ?, *, and – to specify the search pattern. The question mark represents a single character, and the asterisk and hyphen represent zero or more characters. For example, if you are searching for a file containing an address for a company and you are sure that its name began with *South* but do not remember whether its full name is *Southwestern, Southeastern,* or *Southern,* you can enter the word pattern as **South***.

To search for a phrase beginning with one pattern and ending with another, enter it as **"South*Industries"**. This will locate all phrases starting with *South* and ending with *Industries*, such as *Southern Industries, Southwestern Industries, south of the industries*, and so forth. Uppercase and lowercase are considered to be the same.

Using Logical Operators in Searches

Both Versions You can further expand or restrict a word search by using semicolons and blank spaces (which stand for *and*) or commas (which stand for *or*). For example, to search for files that contain both the word *invoice* and the phrase *past due*, you enter **invoice;"past due"**. To search for files that contain either the word *invoice* or the phrase *past due*, enter **invoice,"past due"**.

To search for files that contain either the word *invoice* or the phrase *past due* in combination with the word *October*, enter **invoice,"past due"; October**.

SEE ALSO

Document Summary.

Flush Right

Aligns your text flush with the right margin setting.

SEQUENCE OF STEPS

To align text flush right as you type it:

   Alt-F6 (Flush Right) *or* ⌨ **L**ayout *then* **A**lign *then* **F**lush Right

   ⇒ *<text>* ↵

To align existing text flush right:

Alt-F4 (Block) *or* ▭ **E**dit pull-down *then* **B**lock

➠ *[highlight all lines to be flush right]*

➠ **Alt-F6** (Flush Right) *or* ▭ **L**ayout pull-down *then* **A**lign *then* **F**lush Right

➠ [Just: Right]? **N**o (**Y**es)

USAGE

To align text on the right margin, follow the step sequence shown above. To right-align text after it has been entered, mark the text with Block (Alt-F4) and then select Flush Right (Alt-F6). WordPerfect will prompt you. To have the marked text right-aligned, simply type **Y** for Yes.

To remove the right alignment, locate and delete its code in the Reveal Codes screen.

SEE ALSO

Center.

Font

Allows you to change the size or appearance of the current fonts used in your document.

SEQUENCE OF STEPS

To change the size of a font:

Ctrl-F8 (Font) *then* **S**ize *or* ▭ **F**ont pull-down

➠ Su**p**scrpt; Su**b**scrpt; **F**ine; **S**mall; **L**arge; **V**ry Large; **Ex**t Large

To change the appearance of a font:

> **Ctrl-F8** (Font) *or* 🖱️ **Fo**nt pull-down
>
> ➠ **A**ppearance
>
> ➠ **B**old; **U**ndrln; **D**bl Und; **I**talc; **O**utln; Sh**a**dw; Sm **C**ap; **R**edln; **S**tkout

To return to the initial font defined for the selected printer:

> **Ctrl-F8** (Font) *or* 🖱️ **Fo**nt pull-down
>
> ➠ **N**ormal

USAGE

Font (Ctrl-F8 or the Font pull-down menu) controls a variety of options, all of which affect the way your text appears when printed. This section shows how to enhance the currently selected font by changing either its size or its appearance. For changing the current font, see **Base Font**. For using Font to select colors for printing, see **Print Color**. The options Bold, Undrln, Redln, and Stkout on the Appearance menu are discussed under their own reference entries in this book.

All of the options on the Size and Appearance menus insert a pair of formatting codes and place the cursor between them. You can then enter the text that you want enhanced by the attribute selected. To return to the normal text font, either press the → key once to move the cursor beyond the last code of the pair or select the Normal option on the Font menu (this does the same thing as pressing →). To apply one of these attributes to existing text, mark it as a block using Alt-F4 (Block) before selecting the appropriate Size or Appearance menu option.

To delete any size or appearance attributes assigned to text, locate the pair of codes in the Reveal Codes screen and delete either one of them.

Changing the Size of the Font

The Font menu presents you with seven options. The first two are used for superscripting and subscripting characters.

Superscripted text is printed a half-line above the baseline of the normal text, while subscripted text is printed a half-line below. To change the amount of adjustment up or down, use the Advance feature (see **Advance**) with either option.

The five remaining size options are used to change only the relative size of the current font. The actual point size or pitch used to produce the text that is assigned the attributes Fine, Small, Large, Very Large, and Extra Large depends upon the capabilities of the currently selected printer and the range of fonts installed for that printer.

When you change the size of the text using one of these options, WordPerfect automatically adjusts the line spacing to accommodate the larger or smaller size. To overrule this adjustment, use the Line Height option on the Line Format menu (see **Line Height**).

Changing the Appearance of the Font

When you select the Appearance option on the Font menu, you are presented with nine options to enhance your text. The first two attributes, Bold and Undrln, can also be accessed by pressing F6 or F8 respectively (see **Bold** and **Underline**). The remaining attributes can only be accessed from this menu.

The attributes of double underlining (Dbl Und), italics (Italc), outline, shadow, and small caps can't be produced by every printer. To determine whether your printer can produce these effects, print the PRINTER.TST file that is supplied with the program. If you select an enhancement that your printer doesn't support, WordPerfect will ignore it (unless you have specified italics, in which case the program will substitute underlining).

NOTE

The Small Caps option (Sm Cap) produces all uppercase letters in a smaller font size, a style most commonly used with acronyms and with times (like 9:00 A.M.) When entering text after selecting the Sm Cap option, you don't need to use the Shift key to capitalize the text.

SEE ALSO

Base Font; Bold; Cartridges and Fonts; Line Height; Print Color; Redline/Strikeout; Underline.

Footnotes and Endnotes

Allows you to add footnotes that appear at the bottom of the page or endnotes that appear at a place of your choice in the document.

SEQUENCE OF STEPS

Ctrl-F7 (Footnote) *or* ⌐ᗉ Layout pull-down

➟ **F**ootnote; **E**ndnote; **E**ndnote **P**lacement

➟ **C**reate; **E**dit; **N**ew Number; **O**ptions

USAGE

Notes to the text are automatically numbered for you in WordPerfect. If you want the text of the note to appear on the same page as its reference number, you create a footnote. If you want all of the notes to appear together somewhere in the document, you create an endnote.

The text of footnotes and endnotes is not shown in the text, only their reference numbers. To see the notes before printing, you must use the View Document option on the Print menu (see **View Document**).

Creating Notes

To create a footnote or endnote in the text, follow these steps:

1. Move the cursor to the position where you want the footnote or endnote reference number to appear.

2. Press Footnote (Ctrl-F7) or use the Layout pull-down menu.

3. Select either the Footnote or Endnote option.

4. Select the Create option.

5. Type the text of your note (insert a space between the number on the note editing screen and the text).

6. Press Exit (F7) when you are finished entering the note text.

To delete a footnote or endnote from the document, locate and delete the [Footnote] or [Endnote] code in the Reveal Codes screen.

New Number

WordPerfect automatically begins footnote and endnote numbering from 1. To change the starting number for all notes or to renumber a series of notes from a particular place in the document, use the New Number option on the Footnote or Endnote menu. This feature is especially useful if the document that contains the notes is a subdocument (like a book chapter) of a master document that requires sequential numbering of the notes in all the documents to be printed together (see **Master Document**).

To enter a new starting note number, follow these steps:

1. Move the cursor to the place in the document where the notes are to be renumbered (the top of the document if all notes are to be renumbered).

2. Press Footnote (Ctrl-F7 or choose it from the Layout menu).

3. Select either the Footnote or Endnote option.

4. Select the New Number option.

5. Enter the new starting number and press ↵.

6. Press Screen (Ctrl-F3) and ↵ to renumber notes.

WordPerfect inserts a [New Ftn Num] or [New End Num] code in the document at the cursor's position when you use this option.

Endnote Placement

You can designate where the text of endnotes is to appear by using the Endnote Placement option. If you don't locate the cursor and use Endnote Placement to specify where the endnotes are to be inserted, WordPerfect will automatically place them at the end of your document.

When you use the Endnote Placement option, WordPerfect inserts an [Endnote Placement] code at the cursor's position and prompts you with

Restart endnote numbering? Yes (**No**)

If you choose to restart the endnote numbering from 1, press ↵ to answer Yes to this prompt (WordPerfect inserts the code [New End Num:1] in the document). If you want to retain sequential numbering from the last endnote number, type **N** for No. After you respond to this prompt, WordPerfect inserts the following comment in the text:

Endnote Placement.

It is not known how much space endnotes will occupy here.

Generate to determine.

It also automatically inserts a hard page break after this comment.

To generate the endnotes at this point, select Mark Text (Alt-F5), Generate; select Generate Tables, Indexes, Automatic References, etc.; press ↵; and respond Yes to the prompt:

Existing tables, lists, and indexes will be replaced. Continue? Yes (**No**)

After the endnotes are generated, you will see the comment *Endnote Placement* on the screen. This comment will take up as much space as is required to print all of the endnotes up to that point in the document. To view your endnotes, use the View Document option on the Print menu (Shift-F7).

If you want the text of your endnotes to appear on a new page, be sure to insert a hard page break (Ctrl-↵) before the Endnote Placement comment box.

Changing the Formatting of Notes

When printing your footnotes and endnotes, WordPerfect makes certain assumptions as to how they are to be formatted. You can, however, control their formatting by using Options on the Footnote or Endnote menu.

To change the style of the numbers in the text or note for footnotes or endnotes, select the appropriate options and enter the commands to insert the attributes that you wish to use. Note that you can insert graphics into a note if you select the Character type for the graphics box (see **Graphics**).

When specifying the spacing within footnotes or endnotes, enter **1** for single spacing, **1.5** for one-and-a-half spacing, **2** for double spacing, and so on. You can specify the spacing between notes and the amount of note to keep together on a page by entering a measurement in inches.

When you select the option to change the numbering method for footnotes or endnotes, you are presented with these options:

1 Numbers; **2** Letters; **3** Characters: **0**

When you select Characters, you can specify up to five different characters to be used. After all of the characters you entered are used, WordPerfect will double and then triple them, if necessary.

For footnotes, you may designate that your footnotes be renumbered on each new page or change the type of line separator used to demarcate the footnote from the body of the text. When you select Line Separating Text and Footnotes, you are presented with the options:

1 No Line; **2** 2-inch Line; **3** Margin to Margin

The footnote option Print Continued Messages can be used to have WordPerfect print a *Continued...* message on the last line of any footnote that is split across pages (this message will also be printed on the first line of the note on the following page). You can use the Footnotes at Bottom of Page option (No) to have the footnotes moved up on a short page so that they are printed right under the body of the text rather than at the very bottom of the page with multiple blank lines separating the footnotes from the text.

SEE ALSO

Graphics; Mark Text; Master Document; View Document.

Force Odd/Even Page

Forces the page to be numbered with either an odd or even number.

SEQUENCE OF STEPS

Shift-F8 (Format) *or* ⌐ **L**ayout pull-down

➠ **P**age

➠ **Fo**rce Odd/Even Page

➠ **O**dd; **E**ven

➠ **F7** (Exit)

USAGE

You can use the Force Odd/Even Page feature to ensure that a particular page will always be given either an odd or even page number. To use this command, position the cursor at the top of the page that is always to have either an odd or even page number and follow the step sequence above. When you do, the program inserts either a [Force:Odd] or [Force:Even] formatting code at the cursor's position.

WordPerfect will renumber the page only if Force Odd/Even Page changes it from odd to even or vice-versa.

Any change to the page number is reflected in the Pg indicator on the status line.

Note that the Force Odd/Even Page feature has no effect if you have not specified that some type of page numbering be used in the document (either by issuing the Page Numbering command or by inserting a Page code in a header or footer).

To return to regular page numbering, locate and delete the [Force] code in the Reveal Codes screen.

SEE ALSO

Headers and Footers; Page Numbering.

Forms (5.0)

In version 5.0, the Format and Print menus allow you to set up a form definition and then use it to print all or part of your document.

See **Paper Size/Type** for information about how to use this feature in version 5.1.

SEQUENCE OF STEPS

To define, modify, or delete a form:

Shift-F7 (Print)

➡ **S S**elect Printer

➡ *[highlight printer to print form]*

➡ **E**dit

➡ **Forms**

➡ **A**dd; **D**elete; **E**dit

➡ **F7** (Exit)

To use a form definition:

Shift-F8 (Format)

⟶ **P**age

⟶ **P**aper **S**ize Type

⟶ **F7** (Exit)

USAGE

In version 5.0, you use the Forms option on the Select Printer Forms menu to create a form definition, which stipulates such settings as the paper size and type, orientation, offsets, and location of the paper. You can then apply this form definition to a document by specifying the size and type of paper it uses on the Page Format menu.

WordPerfect comes with three predefined forms: Standard letter size in either portrait (narrow) or landscape (wide) mode, Envelope, and ALL OTHERS (invoked when you try to use a form definition that WordPerfect can't find). You can modify the settings of these forms or add new definitions to the list. To remove a form definition, select the Delete option on the Printer Select: Forms menu.

Creating a Form Definition (5.0)

As indicated by the step sequence, the form definitions that you create are part of the printer definition. When you select the Add option on the Printer Select: Forms menu, you are presented with two full-screen menus—the Form Type menu and the Forms menu. When you select the Edit option, you are presented only with the second Forms menu, where you modify to the selected definition.

When adding a new form definition, you must first specify the type of form to be used. The Form Type menu contains the name of seven frequently used forms. To select one of these, simply enter its mnemonic letter or number. If you want to add your own form description, select Other and enter its name.

After indicating the type of form to be used, you are presented with the Forms menu. Here, you indicate the paper size, orientation of the text on the form, whether or not it is initially present, its location (that is, type of feed or bin number), and any special page offsets to be used.

If you need to modify the size of the form, select the Form Size option. If none of the predefined size options will do, select the Other option and enter the width and length.

To modify the placement of the text on the page, select the Orientation option. You have three choices: Portrait, Landscape, or Both. If you select Portrait, the text will run parallel to the insertion edge of the form. If you select Landscape, it will run perpendicular to the insertion edge. Select Both only when your printer allows you to manually determine the orientation.

The setting of the third option, Initially Present, should be Yes unless the form must be manually fed to the printer.

The Location option determines the type of paper feed; it has three options: Continuous, Bin Number, and Manual.

Use the Page Offsets option when the printhead must be positioned in relation to the top and left edge of the form in the printer. You can enter either positive or negative offsets for the Top and Side settings.

Using a Form Definition (5.0)

To use a form definition to print your document, select the appropriate paper size and type from the Page Format: Paper Size menu, which presents a full-screen menu of common paper sizes.

After you select the paper size, the Paper Type menu appears. To select a named form definition, choose the Other option. This takes you to the Defined Form Types screen, with three options: Select, Other, and Name Search, and an alphabetical list of the forms you have defined. Highlight the appropriate name and type **1** or **S** or press ↵.

If WordPerfect can't match the paper size and type requested against one of the form definitions, you will see the message *requested form is unavailable*. The program will print the document using the paper size specified; however, it will not use any of the formatting instructions attached to the form definition.

Labels; Paper Size/Type.

Go To

Moves the cursor to a specific character, page, or text column, or to the previous cursor position.

SEQUENCE OF STEPS

To go to the next occurrence of a character:

Ctrl-Home (Go To) *or* **S**earch pull-down *then* **G**oto *then* *<character>*

To go to a specific page in the document:

Ctrl-Home (Go To) *or* **S**earch pull-down *then* **G**oto *<page number>* ↵

To return to the previous cursor position:

Ctrl-Home Ctrl-Home

To move the cursor between text columns:

Ctrl-Home (Go To) *or* **S**earch pull-down *then* **G**oto → or ←

USAGE

The Go To feature (Ctrl-Home) is used to move directly to a character or the top of a page. For example, to move to the next occurrence of a hard return (end of paragraph) in the document, you press Ctrl-Home and press the ↵ key. To go to the next period (end of sentence), press Ctrl-Home and type a period. To move directly to the top of a specific page, press Ctrl-Home, type the page number, and press ↵.

To return the cursor to its previous position in the document, press Ctrl-Home twice. This is especially useful when you've moved a block of text to a new place in the document and wish to return immediately to the place from which the block was moved.

SEE ALSO

Cursor Movement.

Go To DOS/Shell

Allows you to exit WordPerfect temporarily to go to DOS or the WordPerfect Library Shell if you run WordPerfect under this utility.

SEQUENCE OF STEPS

Ctrl-F1 (Shell) *or* ⌨ **File** pull-down

➠ **Go** to DOS

➠ DOS **C**ommand

➠ *<DOS command>*

➠ **EXIT** ↵ (to return to WordPerfect)

USAGE

The Go To DOS or Shell feature allows you to leave Word-Perfect temporarily and enter DOS commands while the word processor is still loaded in memory. However, when you go to DOS and try to run another program, you may find that your computer doesn't have sufficient memory to load the new program along with WordPerfect. Also, you should not use this feature to load a RAM-resident utility (sometimes called a TSR) like SideKick. Always exit Word-Perfect before loading this type of software.

When you have finished executing your commands at the DOS prompt and are ready to return to WordPerfect, type the word **EXIT** (don't press the Exit key—F7) and press ⏎. This will return you immediately to the editing screen and any document you have on it.

If you started WordPerfect from the WordPerfect Library shell, you will be returned to the Library Shell menu when you use the Go To DOS feature. From there, you can go to the DOS prompt by selecting the Go to DOS command on the Shell menu (it too uses the key sequence Ctrl-F1 1). When you are finished with DOS, type **EXIT** to return to the Library Shell menu. To return to WordPerfect, type the program letter you have assigned to WordPerfect 5.0.

In Version 5.1, you can also execute one DOS command by choosing DOS Command without leaving WordPerfect. This allows you to write macros that run DOS commands, because WordPerfect is never exited (see **Macros**).

Graphics

Allows you to combine graphics created by other programs with the text of your document or to draw rules in the document.

SEQUENCE OF STEPS

To create or edit a graphics box:

Alt-F9 (Graphics) *or* ◻️ Graphics pull-down

➡ **F**igure; **T**able Box; Text **B**ox; **U**ser Box; **L**ine; **E**quation

➡ **C**reate; **E**dit; **N**ew Number; **O**ptions

Note: In version 5.0, there is no Equation option on the Graphics menu.

To create a Horizontal or Vertical Line graphic:

Alt-F9 (Graphics) *or* ⌐⊳**Graphics pull-down**

➠ Line

➠ Create Line: **H**orizontal; **V**ertical *or* Edit Line: **H**orizontal; **V**ertical

Note: In version 5.0, the line options are **H**orizontal Position; **V**ertical Position; **L**ength of Line; **W**idth of Line; **G**ray Shading (% of black). The Vertical Position option appears only when you are creating a vertical line.

USAGE

You can use Graphics (Alt-F9, or choose **G**raphics from the pull-down menu) to import a variety of illustrations or graphics created with other graphics programs, as well as digitized images created with scanners, and place them directly in your document. In version 5.1, you can use the Graphics feature to import spreadsheets into graphics boxes and to draw vertical and horizontal lines (rules).

To insert a graphic image in a document, you must first create a box to contain it. WordPerfect supports four different box types: Figure boxes for any type of graphic image, Table boxes for tables of numbers, Text boxes for any text that is set off from the body of the document (such as sidebars), and User-Defined boxes for any other type of image. Version 5.1 also provides a special Equation box type for equations (see **Equations**).

You can use graphics boxes in the body of your document and in its headers, footers, footnotes, and endnotes. If you want to insert a graphics box in a style that you are creating (see **Styles**), the box must either be empty or contain only text.

Defining a Graphics Box

After selecting the appropriate type of box for your graphic, select the Create option. The menu options shown on the Definition screen are similar for all types of graphics boxes.

Filename

To retrieve a file that contains text, or an image or graph created with another program, select the Filename option and type in the name of the file, including its extension. Be sure to include the complete path name if the graphics file isn't located in the current directory. Note that you don't have to specify the file at the time you create the graphics box to contain it. You can do this later by choosing the Edit option from the box menu, designating the number, and then choosing the Filename option from the Definition screen.

You can press F5 and ↵ to view the contents of the current directory, or press F5 and enter another directory name to see the contents of that directory. This puts you in the List Files screen, where you can retrieve the file you want (see **List Files**).

Contents

The Contents option, which is new in version 5.1, displays another menu from which you can choose the type of information that you want to put in the graphics box—a graphic image, graphic on disk, text, or equation. Choose the Graphic on Disk option if you want your graphic to be stored in a separate disk file instead of being kept with the document. If you are using the graphic image in a style (see **Styles**), be sure to use this option. Likewise, if you are using one image repeatedly in a document, storing it separately keeps the size of your document down. Selecting Equation and then choosing Edit will automatically display the equation editor (see **Equations**).

Caption

If you want to add a caption to your figure or table, select the Caption option. This brings you to an editing screen much like the ones used to enter headers and footers. The screen contains the name of the box followed by its number. You may delete this text. If you retain the number, it will automatically be updated if you later define or delete graphics boxes (of the same type) that precede it in the document.

Anchor Type

There are three possible types of graphics boxes associated with the Type option: Paragraph, which keeps the graphics box adjacent to the paragraph text; Page, which is affixed to a stationary position on the page; and Character, which is treated like a single character. WordPerfect will always wrap the text of a line that contains a Character box so it is below the boundary of the box, on the next line. Note that Character boxes are the only type that may be added to footnotes and endnotes.

If you select the Page type, you will be asked for the number of pages to skip. If you want the graphics box to remain at a certain position on the page, be sure to locate the cursor at the beginning of the page before you select this option. Then enter **0** if you want the box to appear on the current page, **1** if you want it to appear on the next page, and so forth.

Vertical and Horizontal Position

The Vertical and Horizontal Position options allow you to control the placement of the graphics box on the page. The settings available for them differ according to the type of graphics box chosen.

For the paragraph type, the vertical position setting represents the vertical distance from the first line of the paragraph. The default is 0", which places the graphic even with the paragraph's first line. For the page type, you can align the box vertically with the top or bottom margin, center it on the page, or enter an offset measured from the top edge of the page. If you select Full Page, the graphics box expands to the margin settings for that page. For the character type, you can have the graphics box positioned so that the text of the line it's on is aligned with the top, center, or bottom of the box.

You can position a Paragraph box horizontally so that it aligns with the left or right edge, or is centered between the edges of the area that contains its associated paragraph text. As long as the Wrap Text Around Box option is set to Yes (see below), the text of the paragraph will wrap around the graphics box. In addition, you can have the box fill this entire area from left to right by choosing the Both Left & Right option.

For a Page box, you have three options for setting the horizontal position of the graphics box: Margins, which allows you to left-align, right-align, center, or expand the box to left and right margins; Columns, which allows you to select a text column or range of columns (see **Columns, Text [Newspaper and Parallel]**), using the same alignment options as with Margins; and Set Position, which allows you to position the box a specific measurement in from the left edge of the page. When using the Column option, you can designate a range of text columns by entering their column numbers separated by a hyphen (as in 2–3).

When using the character type of graphics box, you don't need to assign a horizontal position because WordPerfect automatically places the box to the left of the character that contains the cursor at the time you define it.

When you change the vertical position, you can choose Top, Center, or Bottom, or align the baselines. Choose Bottom if what you want is to align the baseline of a graphic image with the line of text that contains its graphics box. Choose Baseline if the box contains an equation and you want to align the equation's baseline with the line of text that contains the box.

Size

Use the Size option to modify the size of the graphics box. When you select this option, you have four choices:

1 Set **W**idth/Auto Height; **2** Set **H**eight/Auto Width;
3 Set **B**oth; **4 A**uto Both

Note: In version 5.0, the **B**oth Width and Height option is equivalent to Set Both, and there is no Auto Both option.

To set both dimensions for the graphics box, select Set Both and then enter the two dimensions. WordPerfect will automatically calculate the opposite dimension if you change the width of the box with the Set Width option or the height with the Height option. Select Auto Both to restore the box's original dimensions.

Wrap Text Around Box

WordPerfect will flow the text around the borders of the graphics box if the Wrap Text Around Box option is set to Yes. On the editing screen, it draws the outline of the graphics box (without displaying the illustration or graph) as you enter the text of the document. If you change this setting to No, the text will go through the graphic and the box outline will not appear on the editing screen. You can preview the positioning of the text around the graphics box by using the View Document feature (see **View Document**).

Edit

Use the Edit option to enter or edit the text for the graphics box or to modify the position or size of an illustration imported from the graphics file designated in the Filename option (see **Filename** above).

When the graphics box contains only text, you can enter or edit as you would any other text in WordPerfect after selecting the Edit option. You can change the font, size, alignment, or attributes of the text by using the appropriate Word-Perfect commands.

When the graphics box contains an illustration or graph created in another program, and you select the Edit option, WordPerfect displays it in graphics mode (if your computer has a graphics card) on the screen surrounded by an outline representing the size and shape of the graphics box that contains it. From here, you can modify its size, its position, or both. Note that you can't add text to an illustration or graph when editing it; this must be done in the program that produced the graphics file.

To move the graphic image in the box, you can press any of the four cursor movement keys. To enlarge the image in the box, press PgUp (or select it from the menu); to shrink it, press PgDn. You can change its proportions by selecting the Scale option and entering a Y-scale (or vertical scale) percentage and an X-scale (horizontal) percentage. To rotate the image clockwise, press the Screen Up key (– on the numeric keypad). To rotate the image counterclockwise, press the Screen Down key (+ on the numeric keypad). You can also rotate the image by selecting the Rotate option and entering the percentage of rotation (where 100% is 360 degrees). When using this option, you can also designate that the image be flipped, by answering Yes to the *Mirror Image?* **No** (**Yes**) question that appears after a percentage is entered.

The % Change option is activated by pressing the Ins (Insert) key. The percentage of change affects the amount that the image is moved, scaled, or rotated when applying the techniques discussed above. You can choose among 1%, 5%, 10%, or 25% change by pressing the Ins key until the percentage you want to use appears in the lower right corner of the screen.

You can use the Invert option on the Edit screen to reverse the image if it is a bitmap graphic rather than a line drawing. When you use it, each white dot (or *pixel*) is changed to black and each black dot to white. Graphics imported from .WPG files (the clip art files included with WordPerfect) and .PIC files (which contain Lotus 1-2-3 graphs) are considered line drawings and, therefore, can't be inverted, while EPS (Encapsulated PostScript) and TIFF (Tagged Image File Format—created by scanners) files can be inverted.

After you have made all the desired modifications to your graphic, press F7 (Exit) to return to the Definition screen. If you want to return the image to the original settings, press the Go To key combination, Ctrl-Home.

Resetting Graphics Box Numbers

WordPerfect numbers each type of graphics box consecutively. You can start a new numbering system at any point in your document by selecting a graphics box type and then choosing New Number. Be sure to position the cursor before the code of the graphics box type where you want to start renumbering.

Because WordPerfect maintains this numbering system for each box type, it can automatically generate a list of your graphics boxes (see **Lists**).

Adjusting the Settings for a Graphics Box

WordPerfect allows you to modify many of the default settings for the graphics boxes you insert in the document. These include the style of the border of the graphics, the inside space between the image and the borders of the box, the outside space between the text and the borders of the box, level numbering methods, the position of the caption, and the gray shading used in the box.

To change any of these settings, move the cursor to the place in the document that contains your graphics box, press Alt-F9 (Graphics) or choose Graphics from the pull-down menu. Select the option that corresponds to the type of box used there, and then select Options. When you change any of the options on this screen, they affect the style of any of the graphics boxes of the same type from the position of the cursor when you made the changes forward in the document.

Creating Horizontal and Vertical Lines

WordPerfect's Graphics feature allows you to create horizontal and vertical lines (rules) of various thicknesses. Use these lines instead of those created with the Line Draw feature when you need to draw rules that use a proportionally spaced font, as lines created with Line Draw will not print correctly unless you are using a monospaced font. To draw a rule in the document, position the cursor on the line where you want the rule to start and follow the key sequence shown at the beginning of this entry.

WordPerfect can draw either a vertical line that extends up and down part of or the entire length of the page or a horizontal line that extends across part of or the entire the width of the page. After selecting the type of line you want, you are presented with line options that allow you to specify the horizontal position (and vertical position if you are creating a vertical line), the length of the line, its thickness, and the amount of gray shading to be applied to it (100% is black).

When specifying the horizontal position of a horizontal line, you can have it aligned with the left or right margin or centered between them. You can also position the line by entering an offset measurement from the left edge of the page or have it extend from the left to the right margin.

When specifying the horizontal position for a vertical line, you can have it drawn slightly ahead of the left margin or after the right margin, or drawn between columns (indicated by number). You can also position the line by entering an offset measurement from the left edge of the page. You can specify the vertical position of the line as centered between the top and bottom margins (Full Page), aligned with either the top or bottom margin, or placed at a specific distance from the top of the page.

Use the Length of Line option to determine how long the rule is to be. If you have specified a horizontal rule whose position is Left and Right, the line length is automatically calculated by the margin settings. For other horizontal lines, the default length (which you can override) is determined by the cursor's position when you created the line.

The Width of Line option allows you to specify how thick the line is to be. To enter this measurement in points, even if the measurement is given in inches by default, follow the number with a *p*.

The Gray Shading option allows you to draw rules in other gradations that are not totally black. To decrease the contrast of the line, enter a percentage (10% is the lowest shading you can specify).

SEE ALSO

Line Draw; Lists; Spreadsheet; View Document.

Hard Return

Terminates paragraphs and short lines or enters blank lines.

SEQUENCE OF STEPS

↵ (Enter)

USAGE

Use the Enter key (↵) to terminate a paragraph of text or a short line that does not extend as far as the right margin, or to add blank lines to a document. When you press ↵, WordPerfect places an invisible hard return in the document, shown by the code [HRt] in the Reveal Codes screen.

When entering the text of a paragraph, you don't need to press ↵ to begin a new line as you do when using a typewriter. WordPerfect automatically wraps text that extends beyond the right margin to the next line. At the end of a line where word wrap occurs, the program inserts a soft return, whose code appears as [SRt] in the Reveal Codes screen.

To separate text into two paragraphs, place the cursor on the first character of the section you want to appear as a new paragraph and press ↵. (It doesn't matter whether you are in Insert or Typeover mode.) To join two paragraphs together, locate the cursor at the beginning of the second paragraph and press the Backspace key to delete the [HRt] code. To use a hard return character that is visible on the screen, use the Edit-Screen options on the Setup menu (version 5.1).

Hard Space

Prevents words from being separated by word wrap.

SEQUENCE OF STEPS

Home-space bar

USAGE

The hard space, entered between two words by pressing the Home key before pressing the space bar, prevents Word-Perfect from separating those words by word wrap. It can be used as the space character in any phrase that should never be separated by word wrap. A hard space code appears as [ ] in the Reveal Codes screen. To convert a hard space to a regular space (subject to word wrap), locate this code, delete it, and press the space bar.

Headers and Footers

Enters running heads at the top or bottom of the pages of your document.

SEQUENCE OF STEPS

Shift-F8 (Format) *or* ⌨ **L**ayout pull-down

➠ **P**age

➠ **H**eaders *or* **F**ooters

➠ Header **A**; Header **B** *or* Footer **A**; Footer **B**

➠ **D**iscontinue; Every **P**age; **O**dd Pages; E**v**en Pages; **E**dit

➡ *[enter or edit text of header or footer]*

➡ **F7** (Exit)

| **USAGE** | ═══════════ |

WordPerfect allows you to create up to two different headers (running heads printed at the top of the page) and two different footers (running heads printed at the bottom of the page) in your document. You can have these headings printed on every page, or just on even or odd pages of the document. Before adding a header or footer to your document (as outlined in the step sequence), position the cursor at the top of the first page on which you want the header or footer to appear.

You can create two headers or footers if you want their text to alternate on even- and odd-numbered pages of a bound document. When using two headers or footers on every page, you can place one flush left and the other flush right or place them on separate lines.

After selecting the number and type of the header or footer you are creating, you are presented with a full editing screen on which to enter the text. You can use as many lines as you need. You can also add any text enhancements (such as boldface or a new font) or formatting (such as centering or flush right). To insert automatic page numbering into your headers and footers, press Ctrl-B (or Ctrl-N) at the position where you want the page number to appear.

Headers begin printing on the first line below the top margin, and WordPerfect places 0.16" between the last line of the header and the body of the text. Footers begin printing on the first line above the bottom margin, and the program places 0.16" between the first line of the footer and the body of the text.

To see how your headers and footers will appear when printed, use the View Document feature. To discontinue a header or footer from a specific page to the end of the document, select the Discontinue option after selecting the appropriate header or footer on the Page menu. To suppress a header or footer on a specific page, use the Suppress (This Page Only) option (see **Suppress Page Format**). To edit the text of a header, select its header or footer number and use the Edit option on the Header or Footer menu. To delete a header or footer, locate and delete the [Header/Footer:] code associated with it. WordPerfect displays the first 50 characters of the header or footer in the Reveal Codes screen.

In version 5.1, you can use columns in headers and footers.

SEE ALSO

Columns, Text (Newspaper and Parallel); Page Numbering; Suppress Page Format; View Document.

Help

Gives you on-line help about a function key or WordPerfect command.

SEQUENCE OF STEPS

To get help on the function keys:

F3 *or* ⌐ꓘ **Help** pull-down *then* **Help** *or* **Index**

➠ *<function key or combination>*

➠ ⏎ *or* **space bar**

To get help on a WordPerfect command:

F3 *or* ⌐ꓘ **Help** pull-down *then* **Help** *or* **Index**

➠ *<first letter of the command>*

➠ ⏎ *or* **space bar**

To display the WordPerfect function key template:

F3 F3 *or* ⌐ꓘ **Help** pull-down *then* **T**emplate

➠ ⏎ *or* **space bar**

USAGE

WordPerfect's on-line help is available any time you are working with the program. To get help about the use of a particular function key or key combination, press F3 (Help), or choose Help or Index from the Help pull-down menu, and then press those function keys. To get help about a particular feature by name, press F3 or use the pull-down sequence indicated, followed by the initial letter of the feature name (such as **S** to get help on Styles). When a letter has more than one Help screen, type **1** (in version 5.0) or the letter itself (in version 5.1) to display another screen of entries for that letter. After locating the name of the feature on the Help screen, press the function keys indicated to obtain information about the feature's use.

Version 5.1 has context-sensitive help. When you are using a particular function, you can get more information about it by pressing F3 or selecting Help from the pull-down menu (when available).

To display a diagram of the function key assignments in WordPerfect, press F3 twice or choose Template from the Help menu if you are using pull-down menus. To exit Help, press ↵ or the space bar (pressing F1—Cancel—simply gives you a screen of help on the Cancel feature).

Hyphenation

Hyphenates words according to WordPerfect's hyphenation rules, either automatically or at your discretion.

SEQUENCE OF STEPS

To turn hyphenation on or off:

Shift-F8 (Format) *or* ⌒ℝ **Layout**

➠ **Line**

➠ **Hyphenation No (Yes)**

⟶ **F7** (Exit)

Note: In version 5.0, the step sequence differs as follows:

⟶ **H**yphenation

⟶ **O**ff; **M**anual; **A**uto

To change the hyphenation zone:

Shift-F8 (Format) *or* ⌐ **L**ayout pull-down

⟶ **L**ine

⟶ **H**yphenation **Z**one Left *<left zone %>* ↵ Right *<right zone %>* ↵

⟶ **F7** (Exit)

USAGE

Versions of WordPerfect prior to 5.1 followed an algorithm (a mathematical "best guess") to determine where to hyphenate a word. Version 5.1 has two hyphenation dictionaries, one internal and one external. The external dictionary is much larger than the internal. You can specify which of these dictionaries to use. If you select the external dictionary, you must have installed the Speller and Thesaurus.

The default setting for WordPerfect's Hyphenation feature is off. To use Hyphenation, you must turn it on. In version 5.0, you must also choose between manual and automatic hyphenation as outlined in the step sequence above.

WordPerfect uses three different types of hyphens:

- Soft hyphens, which the program enters; these are not printed if the document is edited and the word no longer requires hyphenation.

- Hard hyphens, which you enter by pressing the hyphen key (-). These will appear on the screen and in print whenever the word appears. A line can break after a hard hyphen.

- Nonbreaking hyphens, which you specify by pressing Home and then the hyphen key. This prevents a hyphenated word from being split between two lines.

You can insert soft hyphens by pressing Ctrl and the hyphen key or by using the program's Hyphenation feature.

With manual hyphenation (version 5.0), WordPerfect will beep each time a word extends beyond the right margin and starts at or before the left hyphenation zone. You will then see the prompt *Position hyphen; Press ESC.* By pressing Esc, you can see the word as WordPerfect will hyphenate it to the right of this prompt. You can change the place where the word is hyphenated by using the arrow keys to position the hyphen where you want the word to break, and then pressing Esc. If you do not want the word to be hyphenated, press F1 (Cancel).

When automatic hyphenation is on (version 5.0), Word-Perfect will hyphenate any word that starts at or before the hyphenation zone and extends beyond the right margin, without giving you a chance to change the place where it is hyphenated.

The Hyphenation Zone option on the Line format menu is used to change the settings that determine how often Word-Perfect will hyphenate a word. If a word begins before or at the left zone boundary and continues past the right boundary, WordPerfect will either prompt you for a place to insert the hyphen or will immediately hyphenate the word, depending on the type of hyphenation you are using.

The zone boundaries are set as a percentage of the line length. This means that the default setting of 10% for the left boundary is 0.6" and that of 4% for the right boundary is 0.24", if the line length is currently 6". To have WordPerfect hyphenate more frequently, decrease the size of the hyphenation zone. To hyphenate less frequently, increase the size.

→Indent

Sets a temporary left margin and aligns all text to this indent until you press ↵.

SEQUENCE OF STEPS

F4 (→Indent) *or* ⌨ **L**ayout pull-down *then* **A**lign *then* Indent →

➠ <text> ↵

USAGE

For a left indent, select F4 →Indent at the beginning of your paragraph, or choose Align, then Indent → from the Layout menu. The paragraph is then indented 1/2 inch from the left margin, or to the measurement of the first tab stop if you have reset tabs. Select →Indent a second time to indent the paragraph 1 inch (or to the next tab stop), a third time to indent it 1 ½ inches, and so forth. If you select →Indent at the beginning of an existing paragraph, it will be reformatted. If you select →Indent at the beginning of a paragraph you are typing, it will be indented as you type until you press ↵ to signal the beginning of a new paragraph. To indent only the first line in a paragraph, use the Tab key.

To remove an indentation, locate and delete the [→Indent] code in the Reveal Codes screen.

SEE ALSO

→Indent←; Margin Release; Tabs.

→Indent←

Sets temporary left and right margins and aligns all text to these indents until you press ↵.

SEQUENCE OF STEPS

Shift-F4 (→Indent←) *or* ⌨ **L**ayout pull-down *then* **A**lign *then* **I**ndent→←

➠ *<text>* ↵

USAGE

For a left and right indent, select →Indent←. The paragraph will be indented ½ inch from the left and right margins, or to the first tab setting for both sides. Continuing to select →Indent ← will indent the paragraph in increments of 1/2 inch or to the tab settings. To delete a left and right indent, locate and delete the [→Indent←] code in the Reveal Codes screen.

SEE ALSO

→Indent; Tabs.

Indexes

Generates an index from entries marked in the document or stored in a concordance file.

SEQUENCE OF STEPS

To mark an entry for the index:

Alt-F4 (Block) *or* ⌐Edit *then* Block

➡ *[highlight text to be indexed]*

➡ **Alt-F5** (Mark Text) *or* ⌐ **M**ark pull-down

➡ Index

➡ Index Heading: ↵ *or <index heading>* ↵

➡ Subheading: ↵ *or <subheading>* ↵

To define the style of the index:

Alt-F5 (Mark Text) *or* ⌐ **M**ark pull-down

➡ **D**efine

➡ Define Index

➠ Concordance Filename (Enter=none): ↵ or
   <filename> ↵

➠ **No** Page Numbers; **P**age Numbers Follow Entries;
   (Page Numbers) Follow Entries; **F**lush Right Page
   Numbers; Flush Right Page Numbers with **L**eaders

To generate an index:

Alt-F5 (Mark Text) *or* ▭ **M**ark pull-down

➠ **G**enerate

➠ **G**enerate Tables, Indexes, Automatic References, etc.

➠ Existing tables, lists, and indexes will be replaced.
   Continue? Yes (**N**) ↵ *or any key except N*

USAGE

To create an index, you must first mark the items to be included in it, then define its style and generate it. To mark
items for an index:

1. Locate the word or phrase you wish to include in the
   index. Position the cursor on it or on the space following
   it. If you are indexing a phrase, you must first block it by
   pressing Alt-F4 (Block) and highlighting the phrase.

2. Press Alt-F5 (Mark Text) or use the Mark pull-down
   menu and then select the Index option. The prompt *Index
   Heading:* appears. This prompt is followed by the phrase
   you marked or the word the cursor is on. If you want the
   entry to appear in the index just as it does where it is
   highlighted, press ↵. WordPerfect automatically capital-
   izes the first letter of an index heading, and it lowercases
   subheading entries unless the word was capitalized in
   the text. If you want the word or phrase to appear
   differently in the index, type it or edit it as you wish it
   to appear.

3. The program then prompts you for a subheading. If you
   accepted the default word or phrase as the heading,
   you can type a subheading or simply press ↵ for no
   subheading. If you entered a different word or phrase for

the heading, WordPerfect will present that word or phrase as the default subheading. You can press ⏎ to accept it, type over the word WordPerfect presents and substitute the one you wish to use, or delete the subheading if you do not want one.

4. Repeat this process for each word or phrase you want to include in your index.

Creating a Concordance File

A concordance file is simply a list of all the words and phrases that you wish WordPerfect to search for and mark as index entries. To use a concordance file, you specify its file name when you define the style of your index.

To create a concordance file, you need to start a new document and enter the words or phrases you want to use in the index as headings or as subheadings. Press ⏎ after you enter each one. Then, if you are using subheadings, go back and mark each entry with the appropriate index marks by pressing Alt-F5 (Mark Text) or using the Mark pull-down menu and selecting the Index option (you will need to block phrases first). Otherwise, all entries will be headings. You can then generate the index.

Defining the Style of an Index

WordPerfect allows you to choose among several formatting styles for the indexes it generates. To define the style for an index, place the cursor where the index should appear and follow the steps outlined in the step sequence. After you select the Define and Index options, you will be prompted for a concordance file name. Type a name if you are using one; otherwise, press ⏎.

Then select a numbering style from the menu that appears. A [Def Mark] code is inserted in the document when you press F7 (Exit) after selecting a numbering style for the index. This marks the position where the index will be generated. If you want a columnar index, you must insert the column codes and turn the Columns feature on in the text (with Alt-F7) just before the [DefMark:Index] code.

Generating Tables, Lists, and Indexes

After marking the index entries and indicating the style of the index, you are ready to generate the index. Select first the Generate and then the Generate Tables, Indexes, Automatic References, etc. option. You will be prompted that the existing tables, lists, and indexes will be replaced. To have Word-Perfect generate the index, choose **Y** or press any key besides **N**. If you need to save a previously generated index for the document, choose **N**. The index is generated at the [Def Mark] code in the document, and the program automatically inserts an [End Def] mark at the end of the index.

SEE ALSO

Lists; Mark Text; Tables of Contents.

Justification

Specifies the type of justification in the document. In version 5.0, turns on or off right justification only.

SEQUENCE OF STEPS

To specify the type of justification from the function-key menu system in version 5.1:

Shift-F8 (Format)

➡ **Line**

➡ **Justification**

➡ **Left; Center; Right; Full**

➡ **F7** (Exit)

Note: In the pull-down menu system, you select **Layout** then **Justify** to reach the four justification options.

To turn on or off justification in a document (version 5.0):

Shift-F8 (Format)

➠ **Line**

➠ **Justification N** or **Y**

➠ **F7** (Exit)

To compress or expand the word spacing:

Shift-F8 (Format) *or* 🖱 **Layout** pull-down

➠ **Other**

➠ **Printer Functions**

➠ **Word Spacing Justification** Limits

Compressed to (0% – 100%) *<compression %>* ↵

Expanded to (100% – unlimited) *<expansion %>* ↵

➠ **F7** (Exit)

USAGE

By default, full justification (called simply justification in WordPerfect 5.0) is on when you begin a new document. This means that the program will align the right margin of each line by adjusting the spacing between its words. The program can't display justification on the editing screen (the right margin always appears ragged right). To see justification and the spacing between words in each line, use View Document.

You can turn off justification for the entire document (position the cursor at the beginning of the document) or just part of it (position the cursor in the document where you want the change to begin) by following the steps indicated in the step sequence. In version 5.1, you can also turn off justification for all documents by using the Setup menu.

WordPerfect provides two methods for controlling the spacing between words when justification is used. You can turn on WordPerfect's Hyphenation feature and adjust the size of the hyphenation zone (see **Hyphenation**) to reduce the amount of space between words. This is especially useful when you have a short line length, as when using newspaper and parallel columns. You can also adjust the word spacing from the Printer Functions menu (as indicated in the sequence of steps). The Word Spacing Justification option allows you to modify the minimum and maximum range within which WordPerfect can fit justified text. With a proportionally spaced font, the optimal spacing between words is built into the font (expressed by percentage as 100%). Use the Compressed To option to set the minimum word spacing percentage and the Expanded To option to set the maximum word spacing percentage allowed. When one of these limits is reached, WordPerfect begins to adjust the spacing between letters in the words themselves (see **Word/Letter Spacing**).

SEE ALSO

Hyphenation; View Document; Word/Letter Spacing.

Kerning

Turns on or off automatic kerning, which tightens the letter spacing between specific pairs of letters in a font.

SEQUENCE OF STEPS

Shift-F8 (Format) *or* ▭ Layout

➡ **O**ther

➡ **P**rinter Functions

➡ **K**erning **N**o (**Y**es)

➡ **F7** (Exit)

USAGE
Kerning reduces space between specific letter pairs in a font, working from the cursor's position forward in the document.

When you turn kerning on in a document, WordPerfect inserts a [Kern:On] code at the cursor's position. If you decide not to use kerning in the final printed document, locate and delete this code in the Reveal Codes screen.

Version 5.1 allows you to see the letter pairs that are most often kerned in the base font you are using by retrieving the KERN.TST file and printing it.

SEE ALSO
Justification; Word/Letter Spacing.

Labels (Version 5.1)

Allows you to print mailing labels.

SEQUENCE OF STEPS
To set up a mailing label size:

Shift-F8 *or* ⌨ Layout pull-down

➠ **P**age

➠ **P**aper **S**ize/Type

➠ **A**dd

➠ **L**abels

➠ **L**abels **Y**es

➠ Label **S**ize; **N**umber of Labels; Top Left **C**orner; **D**istance between Labels; Label **M**argins ⏎

➠ **F7 F7 F7 F7** (Exit)

To use a defined label size:

> **Shift-F8** *or* ⌨ **L**ayout pull-down
>
> ⮕ **P**age
>
> ⮕ **P**aper **S**ize/Type *[highlight label definition]*
>
> ⮕ **S**elect
>
> ⮕ **F7** (Exit)

USAGE

WordPerfect 5.1 provides a Labels feature to help you set up formats for mailing labels, envelopes, and documents that require special paper sizes and types. (This feature was called Forms in version 5.0.) The program also provides a macro named LABELS that automatically presents you with many standard mailing label sizes from which you can choose directly, without having to set up a special paper size.

When you enter measurements for labels by following the step sequence above, you must be sure to enter accurate dimensions. Enter the width and height of an individual label for the Label Size option. For Number of Labels, enter the number of columns of labels (across) and the number of rows (down). Measure the top left corner on your sheet of labels; if they start at that point, enter 0" and 0" as the measurements. For the Distance Between Labels entry, measure the distance between two labels, not the distance between the top and bottom labels on the page. If there is no space between labels, enter 0" and 0". The Label Margins option lets you enter the left, right, top, and bottom margins for individual labels, not for the entire sheet of labels.

If you are using tractor-fed labels, enter the top left corner measurement as 0", 0". Treat each row of labels as a sheet, so the number of rows is 1 and the number of columns is the number of labels in a row. Enter the paper size as the width of the label. The height should include the distance between the labels.

Once you have set up a paper size for your labels, press F7 twice to return to the Paper Size/Type menu; then select that size by press ↵ with the highlight cursor on the size you want to use. A [Paper Sz/Type:] code will be inserted in your document at that point, and you can begin typing text for the labels. The code must be at the top of the page for it to take effect on that page.

When you type the text of your labels, press Ctrl-⏎ (Page Break) to separate each one.

SEE ALSO

Paper Size/Type; Merge Operations.

Language

Allows you to switch between different language versions of the spelling, thesaurus, and hyphenation dictionaries.

SEQUENCE OF STEPS

Shift-F8 (Format) *or* ▭ **Layout pull-down**

➠ **Other**

➠ **Language** *<language code>* ⏎

➠ **F7** (Exit)

USAGE

WordPerfect comes with an English-language version of the spelling and thesaurus dictionaries. You can, however, purchase foreign language versions of these dictionaries, as well as special hyphenation dictionaries, from WordPerfect Corporation. To have WordPerfect use one of these versions instead of English, you must change the language code default from US (EN in version 5.0) to the appropriate code. With version 5.1, press F3 when your cursor is on the US code (or choose Help from the pull-down menu) to see a list of the codes that WordPerfect uses.

Leading

Allows you to change the amount of white space between lines of text.

SEQUENCE OF STEPS

Shift-F8 (Format) *or* ⌘ Layout

⇒ **O**ther

⇒ **P**rinter Functions

⇒ **L**eading Adjustment

⇒ *<primary leading>* ↵

⇒ *<secondary leading>* ↵

⇒ **F7** (Exit)

USAGE

Leading is the amount of space added between lines of type to make it more readable. WordPerfect normally adds two points of space between lines of text that are set in a proportional font (such as Helvetica or Times Roman), and no leading to lines of text in a nonproportional font (such as Courier) since a fixed amount of leading is built into nonproportional fonts. You can change the amount of leading both between lines of text separated by a soft return and lines separated by a hard return, which begin a new paragraph.

To change the leading you are using, follow the step sequence outlined above, choose Leading Adjustment and enter the amount of space you want to have between lines (Primary) and between paragraphs (Secondary). Since leading is usually measured in points, you may want to enter the value followed by a **p** (such as 4p) if your units of measurement are in inches, which is the default. Otherwise, WordPerfect will interpret the value you enter as a leading specification in inches.

Line Draw

Allows you to draw straight lines and boxes in the document.

SEQUENCE OF STEPS

Ctrl-F3 (Screen) *or* ⌧ **T**ools pull-down

➡ **L**ine Draw

➡ |; ||; *; **C**hange; **E**rase; **M**ove

➡ **F7** (Exit) or **F1** (Cancel)

USAGE

To draw simple graphics in WordPerfect, select Line Draw from either the Screen menu (Ctrl-F3) or the Tools pull-down menu. When you are in WordPerfect's Line Draw mode, the following menu appears:

1 |; **2** ||; **3** *; **4 C**hange; **5 E**rase; **6 M**ove: 1

When you are in Line Draw mode, the option you have selected appears at the end of the menu line. Selecting the first three options allows you to draw single lines, double lines, or asterisks. Selecting Change allows you to choose up to eight different types of alternate drawing characters. In addition, you can use any of the characters that your printer can print (see **Compose**). If you select Erase, the cursor will erase each character it passes through. Selecting Move allows you to move the cursor through your drawing without changing anything.

To enter text in drawings you have created, you should be in Typeover mode. If you remain in Insert mode, which is WordPerfect's default setting, lines will be pushed to the right as you type, and pressing ↵, Tab, or the space bar will insert spaces into your graphics. You can also type text for your graphics first, then enter Line Draw mode and draw lines around the text you have already entered.

To exit Line Draw mode and enter text, press F7 (Exit) or F1 (Cancel). Pressing F1 does not erase any drawings you have created.

NOTE: When creating horizontal and vertical rules for a desktop publishing application, use the Line option on the Graphics menu (Alt-F9), rather than the Line Draw feature.

SEE ALSO

Graphics: Creating Horizontal and Vertical Lines.

Line Height

Allows you to fix the amount of space placed between the baseline of one line and the baseline of the next line in the document.

SEQUENCE OF STEPS

Shift-F8 (Format) *or* ⌧ **L**ayout pull-down

➠ **L**ine

➠ **L**ine **H**eight

➠ **A**uto; **F**ixed *<distance between baselines>* ↵

➠ **F7** (Exit)

USAGE

WordPerfect automatically adjusts the line height—that is, the measurement from the baseline of one line of text to the baseline of the following line of text—to accommodate the largest font used in the line. To override this automatic adjustment and enter a fixed line height for all of the lines in a part or all of the document, use the Line Height option on the Line format menu. After you select Fixed, enter the distance between baselines, measured in points, inches, or centimeters. If you enter the number of points, and inches is the default unit of measurement, be sure to end the number with *p* —WordPerfect will automatically convert this number into corresponding inches.

When you change the line height measurement, WordPerfect inserts a [Ln Height:] code in the document at the cursor's position. The line height will then be changed from that point forward in the document, although the difference in the line spacing will not be visible on the editing screen. (To see the effect that changing the line height has on your text, use View Document.) To return to automatic line height, position the cursor at the beginning of the line where the new line height is to begin, repeat the step sequence, and select the Auto option.

SEE ALSO

Leading; Line Spacing.

Line Numbering

Numbers the lines in the printed version of the document.

SEQUENCE OF STEPS

Shift-F8 (Format) *or* ▭ **Layout**

⮕ **Line**

⮕ **Line Numbering Y**

⮕ **C**ount Blank Lines; **N**umber Every n Lines, where n is; **P**osition of Number from Left Edge; **S**tarting Number; **R**estart Numbering on Each Page

⮕ **F7** (Exit)

USAGE

WordPerfect allows you to specify that lines be automatically numbered in the documents you create. Although the line numbers do not appear on the editing screen, they will be present when your document is printed or when you preview it (see **View Document**).

To number the lines in a document, move the cursor to the first position at the top of the page where you want line numbering to begin. To turn on line numbering at the cursor position, follow the step sequence shown above and type **Y** after choosing the Line Numbering option. To turn line numbering off, type **N** in response to this option. You can also locate and delete the [Ln Num:On] code in the Reveal Codes screen.

When you turn on line numbering, you are presented with five options, which are discussed below.

Count Blank Lines   You can select whether to include blank lines in the line count. If you want blank lines to be skipped, select the Count Blank Lines option and type **N**. WordPerfect automatically includes blank lines as it numbers lines unless you tell it not to. The count does not include blank lines in double-spaced text, however.

Number Every n Lines   Number Every n Lines, where n is allows you to specify the increment for line numbering. For example, if you want to number only every fifth line, enter **5**; WordPerfect will count all the lines but will number only lines 5, 10, 15, 20, and so forth.

Position of Number from Left Edge   The Position of Number from Left Edge option allows you to indicate where you want WordPerfect to print the line numbers. Enter the distance from the left edge of the page in inches.

Starting Number   WordPerfect begins line numbering with 1 on each new page unless you change the Starting Number option and enter a new starting number.

Restart Numbering on Each Page   If you want line numbering to continue sequentially throughout your document, enter **N** for the Restart Number on Each Page option.

SEE ALSO

Outlining; Paragraph Numbering; View Document.

Line Spacing

Allows you to set the line spacing.

SEQUENCE OF STEPS

Shift-F8 (Format) *or* ⌨ Layout

➠ Line

➠ Line **S**pacing *<spacing number>* ↵

➠ **F7** (Exit)

USAGE

The default for WordPerfect is single spacing. To change to another spacing from the cursor's position forward in the document, place the cursor where you want the new spacing to begin and follow the step sequence as shown above. You can enter the spacing number in half-line increments (such as 1.5). WordPerfect displays double spacing (and larger whole number spacing like triple, quadruple, and so on) on the screen. To return to the default of single spacing, locate and delete the [Ln Spacing:] code in the Reveal Codes screen.

SEE ALSO

Leading; Line Height.

List Files

Allows you to obtain an alphabetical listing of all of the files in the current directory and perform common maintenance tasks on them.

SEQUENCE OF STEPS

   F5 (List Files) ↵ *or* ▭ **F**ile pull-down *then* **L**ist Files ↵

➠ **R**etrieve; **D**elete; **M**ove/Rename; **P**rint; **S**hort/Long Display; **L**ook; **O**ther Directory; **C**opy; **F**ind; **N**ame Search

➠ **F1** (Cancel) *or* F7 (Exit) *or* **space bar** *or* zero (0)

Note: In version 5.0, Short/Long Display is replaced by Text In, and Find is replaced by Word Search.

USAGE

List Files (F5) allows you to obtain a directory listing of files, retrieve or print a particular document, or make a new data directory or drive current. In addition, you can carry out many tasks that you would otherwise have to do in DOS, such as deleting and renaming files, creating directories, and copying files to a new disk or directory. For information on using such options on the List Files menu, refer to the individual reference entry in this book under the option name.

When you press F5 or choose List Files from the File pull-down menu, WordPerfect displays the path name of the current directory at the bottom of the editing screen. If you press ↵, it will display a new screen showing an alphabetical list of all program files in that directory as well as the List Files menu.

In version 5.1 you can view an alternate List Files screen called Long Display. The right-hand side of this screen lists files in a directory by their original eight-character DOS names; the left-hand side displays any long document names and document types you have assigned as well as any directory aliases (see **Directories**). To choose Long Display, select Short/Long Display from the List Files menu; then select Long Display. To return to the short display, select Short Display. To retrieve a document by using its long document name, you must use the List Files screen. See **Short/Long Document Display** for more information about Long Display and document types.

To move through the list of file names on the List Files screen, use the ↑, ↓, PgUp, and PgDn keys. To move directly to the last file name in the list, press Home Home ↓. To move to the first file, press Home Home ↑. To move between columns, use the ← and → keys.

To locate a particular file quickly, type **N** and start typing the first few characters of its name to activate the Name Search feature. The program tries to match the letters entered with files in the listing and moves the highlight directly to the first match. Press ↵ or one of the arrow keys to exit from Name Search.

To view the contents of a different directory, edit the displayed path name or enter another path name. If you will be working in a different directory during the current session, you can change the default directory (see **Directories**). Once you have made a particular directory current, all of the documents you create and save will automatically be located in it.

Press Esc, F1 (Cancel), 0, or F7 (Exit) to return to your document after viewing the List Files screen.

In WordPerfect 5.1, you can press F5 (List Files) to display the contents of a directory when you are importing a spreadsheet (see **Spreadsheet**) and when you are retrieving a graphic image (see **Graphics**).

Looking at the Contents of Files and Directories

The Look option is the default setting on the List Files menu. It allows you to display the contents of the file whose name is currently highlighted. This feature is helpful when you need to view the contents of a file to see if it is the document you want to edit or print.

When you highlight the name of a file and press ↵ (or choose the Look option), WordPerfect displays the first part of the document on the screen. If you have added a document summary to the file, you will see its statistics at the top of the screen. You can scroll through the document using any of the standard cursor keys. To view the next or previous file in the directory listing, choose Next Doc or Previous Doc.

In version 5.1, if the file you are looking at has a document summary, it will be displayed first, and you will see the following menu:

1 Next; **2 P**revious; **3 L**ook at Text, **4 P**rint Summary;
5 Save to File

Choose Look at Text to look at the text of the document. To print the summary, choose Print Summary; you can also save it as a separate file by choosing Save to File. To return to the List Files menu after viewing the contents of the file, press F7 (Exit).

You can also use the Look option to temporarily view a new directory and locate the documents listed there. Highlight the name of the directory whose listing you wish to see and press ↵ (or choose Look and press ↵), or double-click with the mouse.

SEE ALSO

Copying Files; Deleting Files; Directories; Document Summary; Find; Name Search; Printing; Retrieve; Short/Long Document Names; Text In/Out (version 5.0).

Lists

Generates lists of figures, tables, and so on, from marked entries in your document.

SEQUENCE OF STEPS

To mark an entry for the list:

Alt-F4 (Block) *or* ⌐ᗺ **E**dit pull-down *then* **B**lock

⮕ *[highlight text to be listed]*

⮕ **Alt-F5** (Mark Text) *or* ⌐ᗺ **M**ark pull-down

⮕ **L**ist

⮕ *<list number between 1 and 5>*

To define the style of the list:

Alt-F5 (Mark Text) *or* ⌐ᗺ **M**ark pull-down

⮕ **D**efine

⮕ Define **L**ist

⮕ *<list number>*

⮕ **N**o Page Numbers; **P**age Numbers Follow Entries; (Page Numbers) Follow Entries; **F**lush Right Page Numbers; Flush Right Page Numbes with **L**eaders

To generate a list:

Alt-F5 (Mark Text) *or* ⌐ᗺ **M**ark pull-down

⮕ **G**enerate

⮕ **G**enerate Tables, Indexes, Automatic References, etc.

⮕ Existing tables, lists, and indexes will be replaced. Continue? **Y**es (**N**o) ↵ *or any key except N*

USAGE

You can mark up to five separate lists in a document, but an item may belong to only one list. For each item that you want to include in a list, follow these steps:

1. Press Alt-F4 (or choose Block from the Edit menu) and use the cursor movement keys or the mouse to mark the list item as a block.

2. Press Alt-F5 (Mark Text), then select the List option.

3. When the *List*# prompt appears, enter the number of the list (from 1 to 5).

When you mark a list entry with this method, Word-Perfect places [Mark:List,#] and [End Mark:List,#] codes around the marked text. To delete the entry from the list, you need only to locate and delete the [Mark:List #] code for that entry in the Reveal Codes screen.

In addition to the five lists you mark yourself, Word-Perfect automatically maintains separate predefined lists of the captions for figures, tables, text boxes, user-defined boxes, and equations (version 5.1) created with the Graphics feature (see **Graphics**); they are assigned the list numbers 6 through 10, respectively. For example, to create a list composed of all of the captions for the text boxes in a document, you simply define the style and generate list 8. There is no need to mark individual captions.

Defining the Style of the List

WordPerfect allows you to choose among several formatting styles for the lists it generates. To define the style for a list, follow the steps as outlined in the step sequence. After you select the Define and List options and indicate the number of the list (1–10), you select the option number corresponding to the style you wish to use.

A [Def Mark:] code is inserted in the document when you press F7 (Exit) after selecting a style for the list. This marks the position where the list will be generated. Therefore, most often you will want to position the cursor at the end of the document before you define the list style to have it generated there.

Generating Tables, Lists, and Indexes

After marking the list entries (if you are creating a list from 1–5) and indicating the style of the list, you are ready to generate it. After selecting the Generate and Generate Tables, Indexes, Automatic References, etc. options, you will be prompted that existing tables, lists, and indexes will be replaced.

To have WordPerfect generate the list, choose **Y** or press any key besides **N**. If you have previously generated an index for the document, it will be completely replaced unless you choose **N**. The list is generated at the [Def Mark] code in the document, and the program automatically inserts an [End Def] mark at the end of the list.

SEE ALSO

Graphics; Mark Text.

Locking a File

Allows you to protect a document with a password.

SEQUENCE OF STEPS

To add or change a password:

Ctrl-F5 (Text In/Out) *then* **P**assword *or* ⌐ **File** pull-down *then* **Pass**word

➥ **A**dd/Change

➥ *<password>* ↵

➥ *<password>* ↵

To delete password protection:

Ctrl-F5 (Text In/Out) *then* **P**assword *or* ⌒ᗩ **File**
pull-down *then* **P**assword

➠ **R**emove

USAGE

To lock the file displayed on the screen, follow the step sequence above and select Add/Change. You will then be
prompted to enter the password twice. The password can
contain up to 24 characters. WordPerfect does not display
the password on the screen, so it asks you to enter it twice to
protect against typing errors. If the password you enter is
not the same each time, you will receive an error message
and must begin the file-locking procedure again.

As soon as you save the document after assigning a
password, it will be saved with the document. Thereafter,
you will have to enter the password in order to retrieve,
copy, move, or rename the document as well as to print it
from disk. If you aren't able to enter the password correctly,
you will not be able to retrieve or print it ever again.

Once you have retrieved a locked file, you can edit it just
like any other WordPerfect document. To remove a password from a file after retrieving, press Ctrl-F5 (Text In/Out)
and select Password; then Remove. The next time you save
the document, it will be saved without the password, which
will no longer be required when you retrieve the file or print
it from disk.

Macros

Enables you to record keystrokes and replay them at any time by entering the macro name under which they are stored.

SEQUENCE OF STEPS

To define a macro:

Ctrl-F10 (Macro Define) *or* ⌐ **Tools** pull-down *then* **Macro** *then* **Define**

➠ *<macro name>* ↵

➠ *<description of macro>* ↵

➠ *<keystrokes to be recorded>* ↵

➠ **Ctrl-F10** (Macro Define)

To edit an existing macro:

Ctrl-F10 (Macro Define) *or* ⌐ **Tools** pull-down *then* **Macro** *then* **Define**

➠ *<macro name>* ↵

➠ **Edit**

➠ *[change keystrokes, commands]*

➠ **F7** (Exit)

To replace an existing macro:

Ctrl-F10 (Macro Define) *or* ⌐ **Tools** pull-down *then* **Macro** *then* **Define**

➠ *<macro name>* ↵

➠ **Replace Y**

➠ *<new description of macro>* ↵

➠ *<new keystrokes to be recorded>*

➠ **Ctrl-F10** (Macro Define)

To execute an Alt-key macro:

Alt-<*letter assigned to macro*>

To execute all other macros:

Alt-F10 (Macro) *or* ⌨ **T**ools *then* **M**acro *then* **E**xecute

➠ *<macro name>* ↵

| USAGE |

A macro is a recorded sequence of keystrokes that you save in a file and can use repeatedly. Macros can consist of text that you do not want to retype, such as standard paragraphs in a contract or form letter, or complex sequences of commands, such as those that set up a document's format, save the document, and print it. You can even combine text and commands within macros to automate repetitious procedures such as locating and replacing formatting codes throughout a document.

You can set up macros that repeat themselves, as well as macros that call other macros. In addition, you can specify that a macro be executed only if a certain condition is met.

The subject of macros is extensive, and it is beyond the scope of this *Instant Reference* to teach you how to use macros. Consult Kay Nelson's *WordPerfect 5 Macro Handbook* for suggestions about using macros in your work, a discussion of the sophisticated macro command language, and a library of working macros.

Creating Macros

This section presents the rules you need to follow while creating macros.

To create a macro:

1. Select Macro Define to begin the macro definition. Word-Perfect will display the prompt *Define Macro:*. Enter a

macro name from one to eight characters long, with no spaces between characters, followed by ↵, or press the Alt key in combination with a letter from **A** to **Z**, or simply press the Enter key (↵).

2. WordPerfect will then display the prompt *Description:*. You may then enter a description of the macro's function, if you wish. It can consist of up to 39 characters. Then press ↵.

3. WordPerfect then displays the prompt *Macro Def*, which you'll see at the bottom of the screen until you terminate the macro definition. Enter all of the keystrokes that you want to include in the macro. Do not use the mouse to position the cursor in text; use the cursor keys instead.

4. Select Macro Define a second time to terminate the macro definition. WordPerfect automatically saves the definition in a file. The program appends the extension .WPM to the end of the file name you assigned to the macro. Macro files are automatically saved in the directory that you indicate as the Keyboard/Macro Files directory or in the directory that contains the WordPerfect program files, if you haven't yet specified such a directory.

Executing Macros

To execute a macro whose name consists of one to eight characters, select Alt-F10 or select Macro *then* Execute from the Tools pull-down menu. WordPerfect displays the prompt *Macro:*. Enter the name of the macro and press ↵.

To execute a macro that uses the Alt key and a letter from A to Z, you simply press Alt in combination with the letter key you assigned to the macro.

To execute a macro that was named with the Enter key (↵), press Alt-F10 and press ↵. To terminate any macro before it is finished, press F1 (Cancel).

Replacing and Editing Macros

If a macro that you have defined does not work as you intended, you can redefine or edit it. To do either, select Macro Define and enter the same name you used when you originally defined the macro. WordPerfect 5.1 will display the prompt

<macro name>.WPM is Already Defined. **1 R**eplace;
2 Edit: **0**; **3 D**escription

where *macro name* is the name you entered (version 5.0 does not have the Description option). To redefine the macro, select the Replace option, respond **Y**es to the prompt, and reenter a new description and the keystrokes you want recorded. Press Ctrl-F10 to terminate and save the new definition when you are finished.

To edit the contents of a macro, select the Edit option. This takes you to the Macro Editor and places the cursor inside the macro editing window which displays the keystrokes already saved in the macro.

In WordPerfect 5.0, the Macro Editor has two options, Description and Action. To change the macro's description, select the Description option, edit the comment line, and press ↵. To edit the contents of the macro, select the Action option.

Macro programming commands and standard Word-Perfect editing commands entered into the macro are both represented by a command or feature name enclosed in a pair of braces. For example, you might see the macro command {BELL}, which sounds the bell, or the editing command {Underline}, which underlines text.

To move the cursor, insert new text, or delete existing text or codes in the Macro Editor, use the WordPerfect editing and cursor movement keys as usual. However, to add new WordPerfect commands to the macro, you must press Ctrl-V or Ctrl-F10 (Macro Define) before you press the appropriate function key(s). If you use Ctrl-F10 to enter the Function Key mode, you must press it again to reenter Edit mode before you use any of the editing or cursor movement keys. Otherwise, WordPerfect will insert their codes into the macro (such as {Left} when you press ←) rather than performing their usual function (to move the cursor one character to the left). To insert a macro programming command in a macro, press Ctrl-PgUp. This displays a list of programming commands that you can scroll through. Move the highlight cursor to the command you wish to use and press ↵ to insert it into the macro.

Once you have finished editing the contents of a macro, press F7 (Exit) to save the new definition and return to the document editing screen. Press F1 (Cancel) if you wish to abandon any editing to the macro.

Enhancing Macros

You can insert a pause into a macro so that you can enter data from the keyboard while the macro is being executed. This makes it possible to write a "general" macro that can be used to accept variable data.

To enter a pause for input into a macro, begin the definition of the macro as described above and then press Ctrl-PgUp at the point where you want to insert the pause. The following menu options will appear at the bottom of the screen:

1 Pause; **2 D**isplay; **3 A**ssign; **4** Comment: **0**

Select Pause and then press ↵ and continue with the definition of your macro. When you execute a macro that contains a pause (or pauses) for input, the macro will execute all keystrokes up to the place where you entered the pause and then beep to signal that it has paused. To resume macro execution after you have entered your text, press ↵.

To make a macro's operation visible on the screen, select the Display option after pressing Ctrl-PgUp. The prompt *Display execution? No (Yes)* will appear on the screen. Type **Y** to have the menu options briefly displayed on the document editing screen as WordPerfect commands are selected.

Chaining Macros

A macro can be started from within another macro, or a macro can be made to loop continuously by calling itself. To chain one macro to another, enter the second macro's name at the end of the first macro by pressing Alt-F10 followed by the name of the macro (if you are chaining an Alt macro, you must still press Alt-F10 before pressing Alt and the appropriate letter). When two macros are chained together in this way, all of the keystrokes in the first macro are executed before the keystrokes in the second are executed. By including a search procedure that locates text that you want the macro to process, you can make a macro automatically repeat until it has operated on all occurrences of the search string.

Nesting Macros

You can nest an Alt macro inside another macro by pressing Alt followed by the appropriate letter key (this time, don't press Alt-F10 before you press Alt and the letter key). When an Alt macro is nested inside another macro, WordPerfect executes the Alt macro's commands as soon as it comes to its name in the sequence of executing the commands in the first macro. After all of the commands in the Alt macro have been executed, WordPerfect resumes execution of any commands that come after the Alt macro name in the original macro.

Note: WordPerfect 5.0 macros will run under WordPerfect 5.1 if the keystrokes are the same; however, option numbers in some menus have changed. For example, some of the options on the Setup menu (Shift-F1) and the List Files screen (F5) have been renumbered, as has the option for the path for downloadable fonts. If your 5.0 macro behaves erratically, edit it in the macro editor to conform to the new key sequence.

Margin Release

Moves the cursor one tab stop to the left of the left margin.

SEQUENCE OF STEPS

To release the margin:

Shift-Tab (Margin Release) *or* ⌐ᴀ **L**ayout
pull-down *then* **A**lign *then* **M**argin Rel←

To create a hanging indentation:

F4 (→Indent) **Shift-Tab** (Margin Release) *or* ⌐ᴀ
Layout pull-down *then* **A**lign *then* **I**ndent→ *then*
Layout *then* **A**lign *then* **M**argin Rel←

USAGE

To move the cursor one tab stop to the right, press the Tab key. To move the cursor one tab stop to the left, select Margin Release. When you use Margin Release to move left, Word-Perfect inserts a [←Mar Rel] code in the document in front of the [Tab] code. If you delete the [←Mar Rel] code, only, the [Tab] code will remain, and any text will be indented to its stop.

You can use Margin Release with Indent to create a hanging indentation. To do this, press F4 to indent the paragraph and then press Shift-Tab to remove the indentation for the first line only. Succeeding lines will be indented, as in the following example:

Hanging indents are often useful to call attention to paragraphs in a series. Sometimes this style of indentation is referred to as an *outdent*.

You can delete a hanging indentation, locate and delete the [←Mar Rel] and [→Indent] codes in the Reveal Codes screen.

SEE ALSO

Flush Right; →Indent; →Indent←; Tabs; Tab Align.

Margins, Left and Right

Allows you to change the left and right margins of your document.

SEQUENCE OF STEPS

Shift-F8 (Format) *or* ⌧ **L**ayout pull-down

➠ **Line**

➠ **M**argins: Left *<distance from left edge>* ↵; Right *<distance from right edge>* ↵

➠ **F7** (Exit)

USAGE

To change the left and right margins for a document, position the cursor at the beginning of the line where you want the new margins to begin and follow the step sequence. The left margin setting is the distance from the left edge of the paper, and the right margin setting is the distance from the right edge of the paper. Any change to these settings takes effect from the cursor's position forward in the document. To set new left and right margins for the entire document, be sure that the cursor is at the beginning of the file (press Home Home ↑ to get there) before you change them.

When you change the left and right margin settings in a document, WordPerfect inserts an [L/R Mar:] code that includes their new settings. To revert to the default 1" settings, locate this code in the Reveal Codes screen and delete it.

SEE ALSO

Forms (version 5.0); Margins, Top and Bottom; Paper Size/Type.

Margins, Top and Bottom

Allows you to change the top and bottom margins of your document.

SEQUENCE OF STEPS

Shift-F8 (Format) ⌨ Layout pull-down

➠ **P**age

➠ **M**argins: Top *<distance from top edge>* ↵; Bottom *<distance from bottom edge>* ↵

➠ **F7** (Exit)

USAGE

To change the top and bottom margins for a document, position the cursor at the beginning of the page where you want the margins to change and follow the step sequence. The top margin setting is the distance from the top edge of the paper and the bottom margin setting is the distance from the bottom edge of the paper. Any change to these settings takes effect from the cursor's position forward in the document. To set new top and bottom margins for the entire document, be sure that the cursor is at the beginning of the file (press Home Home ↑ to get there) before you change them.

WordPerfect maintains the top and bottom margin settings in effect by automatically adjusting the number of lines per page according to the fonts and line heights used. Therefore, there is no need to change the top and bottom margin settings when you change the sizes of fonts or the line height(s) in the document.

When you change the top and bottom margin settings in a document, WordPerfect inserts a [T/B Mar:] code that includes their new settings. To revert to the default top and bottom margin settings of 1" each, locate and delete this code in the Reveal Codes screen.

SEE ALSO

Forms (version 5.0); Line Height; Margins, Left and Right; Paper Size/Type.

Mark Text

Compares documents, removes redline markings and strikeout text, and creates automatic references, master documents, indexes, lists, tables of authorities, and tables of contents.

SEQUENCE OF STEPS

To access the Mark Text menu:

Alt-F5 (Mark Text) *or* ⊂ʰ Mark

➠ Cross **R**ef; **S**ubdoc; **I**ndex; To**A** Short Form; **D**efine; **G**enerate

To mark a table of contents, list, index, or table of authorities reference:

Alt-F4 (Block) *then [highlight text to be marked] then* **Alt-F5** (Mark Text) *or* ⊂ʰ **M**ark

➠ To**C**; **L**ist; **I**ndex; To**A**

USAGE

Mark Text is used for automatic references, master documents, document comparison, redline and strikeout removal, outlining, paragraph numbering, indexes and concordances, and tables of contents and authorities. When you press Alt-F5, or use the Mark pull-down menu, you will see the options shown at the top of the step sequence section. (If you're using the pull-down menu system, you will also see the options Master Documents and Document Compare.) If you have already marked text as a block, the options are slightly different (as shown at the bottom of the step sequence section), because they are designed to allow you to designate which category the marked text is to be in.

For specific information on how Mark Text is used in WordPerfect, refer to the individual reference entries shown in the See Also section below.

SEE ALSO

Cross-Reference; Document Compare; Indexes; Lists; Master Document; Redline/Strikeout; Tables of Authorities; Tables of Contents.

Master Document

Allows you to create a master document containing separate documents (specified as subdocuments) that are to be printed together.

SEQUENCE OF STEPS

To insert a subdocument in the master document:

Alt-F5 (Mark Text) *or* ⌨ **M**ark pull-down

➡ **S**ubdoc

➡ *<name of file to be inserted>* ↵

To expand the master document:

Alt-F5 (Mark Text) *or* ⌨ **M**ark pull-down

➠ **G**enerate

➠ **E**xpand Master Document

To condense the master document:

Alt-F5 (Mark Text) *or* ⌨ **M**ark pull-down

➠ **G**enerate

➠ **C**ondense Master Document

➠ **S**ave Subdocs? **No** (**Yes**)

USAGE

The Master Document feature allows you to join any number of separate WordPerfect files together so that they are treated as one long document for the purposes of printing and automated references.

Each WordPerfect document tied to a master document is considered a subdocument. A master document may be simply a series of subdocument codes, indicating where the text of each subdocument is to be inserted, or it may contain text of its own. To insert a subdocument code, position the cursor in the master document where the subdocument text is to occur (usually pressing Ctrl-↵ first to ensure that it begins on a separate page) and follow the step sequence above. When prompted to enter the subdocument file name, type the name of the document. When you press ↵, Word-Perfect displays the name of the subdocument, enclosed in a single-line box, and enters a [Subdoc:] code into the master document. To delete a subdocument from a master document, locate this code in the Reveal Codes screen and delete it—the box containing the subdocument's name in the document editing screen will then disappear.

Expanding and Condensing Subdocuments   To edit the text of a subdocument from within the master document, expand the master document to include the text of all subdocuments within it. Just follow the steps outlined in the step sequence section.

When the master document is expanded, the [Subdoc:] code is replaced by the text of the subdocument, enclosed in

[Subdoc Start:] and [Subdoc End:] codes. Once a master document is expanded, you can edit any of its text, including that within the [Subdoc Start:] and [Subdoc End:] codes.

When you use the Exit (F7) or Save (F10) functions on an expanded master document, you receive the prompt *Document is expanded, Condense it? Yes (No)*. Press ↵ to condense it before saving it. When you condense a master document, as indicated in the step sequence, the text of the subdocuments is replaced with the appropriate [Subdoc:] codes. Choose No to save it in expanded form. If you press ↵, you receive a second prompt *Save Subdocs? Yes (No)*. In version 5.1 you have three options: choose Yes to have WordPerfect replace the subdocument with its revised version; choose No to save the subdocument under a new file name; choose Replace All Remaining to save all the revised subdocuments in the master document without further prompts.

Press ↵ to save any editing changes in the subdocument files before the master document is condensed. Choose N if you don't want to update the subdocuments with the changes you have made.

You can also condense a master document at any time before saving it. When you do, you receive the same prompt to save the subdocuments as when you save the master document.

During editing, be careful that you don't delete any of the [Subdoc Start:] or [Subdoc End:] codes. If you do, Word-Perfect won't be able to replace the text that belongs to those codes with the [Subdoc:] code. Therefore, the subdocument's text will remain expanded in the master document. In such a case, delete the subdocument text that can't be condensed and then reinsert the file as a subdocument.

You must expand the master document before you print it, or the printout will contain the Subdocument codes instead of the text stored in the subdocuments.

You should also expand prior to generating tables of contents, lists, and indexes. WordPerfect will automatically expand it for you and display the prompt *Update Subdocs? Yes (No)*. Press ↵ to save the subdocuments before condensing the master document. Choose N if you don't want the changes saved to them.

SEE ALSO

Indexes; Lists; Tables of Contents.

Math

Performs calculations on numbers in your document.

SEQUENCE OF STEPS

To turn the Math feature on and off:

Alt-F7 (Columns/Tables) *or* ⌐ Layout pull-down **M**ath
➠ **O**n/Off

To define math columns:

Alt-F7 (Columns/Tables) *then* **M**ath *then* **D**efine *or* ⌐
Layout pull-down *then* **M**ath *then* Math **D**ef

➠ *<type of columns, negative number display, number of decimal places, and formulas to be used>*

➠ **F7** (Exit)

Note: In version 5.0 the Columns/Table key is called the Math/Columns key.

USAGE

You can use WordPerfect as a calculator for simple mathematical functions such as addition, subtraction, multiplication, and division. The program can calculate totals, subtotals, and grand totals on numbers down columns. In addition, you can write formulas that perform mathematical operations across columns of numbers.

You can use the Tables feature of version 5.1 much like a spreadsheet (see **Tables**). You may want to use Tables instead of the Math feature for some applications.

Turning Math On

To get totals, subtotals, and grand totals from simple columns of numbers (not predefined as Math columns):

1. Clear and then reset the tabs (see **Tabs**). When Math mode is on, WordPerfect will align tabs on the decimal/alignment character, which is the period (.) unless you change it (see **Decimal/Align Character**).

2. To turn Math on, press Alt-F7 (Columns/Tables), select the Math On option, and then select On. The *Math* prompt appears in the lower left corner of the screen.

3. Press the Tab key to move to the first column, then enter the numbers you wish to work with. When you press the period (.) to indicate a decimal point, the numbers will align on that decimal point. When Math mode is on, WordPerfect treats the tab stop as a decimal tab, like the Tab Align key.

4. Wherever you want a subtotal to be calculated in that column, insert a plus sign (+), either from the numeric keypad or from the top row of your keyboard. Word-Perfect will subtotal each number in the column after the previous plus sign. Where you want a total of the subtotals, enter an equal sign (=). If you want any numbers to be considered as subtotals or totals even if no calculation has been performed on them, enter **t** before any additional subtotals and **T** before any additional totals. To calculate a grand total—the total of all the totals — enter an asterisk (*).

5. To tell WordPerfect to make the calculations you have specified, select Columns/Tables and then Calculate. (You can select this option at any time to have the program perform calculations —for example, as you enter the numbers.) WordPerfect displays double question marks (*??*) if it cannot make a calculation. If this occurs, recheck your Math Definition screen to make sure that the column references in any formulas you have written are correct.

6. Turn Math mode off by selecting Math Off from the Columns/Tables menu.

When Math mode is on, you can move between columns by using a combination of the Ctrl key and the → and ← keys. Pressing Home ← after the Ctrl-Home (Go To) sequence takes you to the beginning of the first text column.

Defining Math Columns

If you want to perform calculations across columns of numbers, you need to define math columns.

For each column, you define three things: the type of column (calculation, text, numeric, or total), the symbol to be used with negative numbers (either parentheses or the minus sign), and the number of decimal places that are to be displayed (0–4). To do this, press Alt-F7 and select the Math Def option to use the Math Definition screen, or select Math from the Layout Menu; then select Define. Each row under the letters A through X corresponds to a column.

All columns are predefined as numeric columns (type 2). To change a column's definition, move the cursor to its letter by using the arrow keys. Enter 0 if the column is to contain a formula, enter 1 if the column is to contain only text, and enter 3 if the column is to contain a total calculated from other columns. If you have defined the column as type 0, the cursor moves down to the Calculation Formulas section of the screen to allow you to enter the formula for the calculation. Only four columns can be defined for calculations. Press F7 to exit to the menu and save the definition. Press F1 to cancel.

Displaying Totals in Separate Columns

If you have defined Math columns, you can display subtotals, totals, and grand totals in separate columns. To do so, simply define the column or columns that you wish to hold the total calculations as total columns (type 3) and type the

+, =, or * symbol in your document in the column where you want the calculation to appear.

Using Special Operators for Row Calculations

To use certain special operators in computing the totals and averages of rows, define the column that is to hold these special operators as a calculation column (type 0). Then, when the cursor moves to the Calculation Formulas area of the Math Definition screen, enter any one of the special operators listed here.

- The + symbol calculates the total of all the numbers in the row that are in numeric columns (type 2).

- The +/ symbol calculates the average of all the numbers in the row that are in numeric columns (type 2).

- The = symbol calculates the total of all the numbers in the row that are in total columns (type 3).

- The =/ symbol calculates the average of all the numbers in the row that are in total columns (type 3).

These special operators work on numbers to their right and left, across the entire row—not just on numbers to the left.

Revising Math Definitions

You will often want to change the definitions of math columns so that you can add new columns of data, delete columns, or move columns to new locations. With your cursor positioned before the [Math On] code in the Reveal Codes screen, you can delete the old [Math Def] code. Then press Alt-F7 (Columns/Tables) and select the Math Def option to change any column definitions that you wish. Recalculate by using the new definition before you move to another part of your document.

To revise a Math Definitions screen that you have already defined, position the cursor to the right of the [MathDef] code before you press Alt-F7 and select the Math Def option. You can then use the cursor movement keys to position the cursor on the settings you wish to change. To edit a formula, place the cursor on the *0* that defines the column holding the formula and reenter **0**. The cursor will move to the Calculation Formulas section of the screen, where you can edit the formula or delete it by pressing F1 (Cancel).

Remember that if you add, delete, or move columns, you will also need to revise the formulas that involve them.

SEE ALSO

Decimal/Align Character; Tables; Tabs.

Merge Operations

Merges data stored in lists in a secondary document into the appropriate places in a primary document.

SEQUENCE OF STEPS

To designate a field from the secondary file to be merged in the primary file:

> **Shift-F9** (Merge Codes) *or* ◁ **Tools** pull-down *then* Merge Codes
>
> ➠ Field
>
> ➠ Field: *<enter field number>* ↵

To insert other Merge codes:

> **Shift-F9** (Merge Codes) or ◁**Tools** *then* Merge Codes
>
> ➠ Field; **E**nd Record; **I**nput; **P**age Off; **N**ext Record; **M**ore

To separate fields in the secondary file:

> **F9** (End Field)

To separate records in the secondary file:

> **Shift-F9** (Merge Codes) *or* ⌐ **T**ools pull-down *then* **Merge Codes**
>
> ➠ **End Record**

To perform a merge:

> **Ctrl-F9** (Merge/Sort) *or* ⌐ **T**ools pull-down
>
> ➠ **Merge**
>
> ➠ Primary File: *<name of primary file>* ↵
>
> ➠ Secondary File: *<name of secondary file>* ↵

Note: Merge codes have changed in version 5.1 of Word-Perfect. In version 5.0, you enter the merge codes ^C, ^D, ^E, ^F, ^G, ^N, ^O, ^P, ^Q, ^S, ^T, ^U, and ^V by pressing Shift-F9. Ends of fields are indicated by pressing F9. Ends of records are indicated by pressing Shift-F9 and inserting a ^E merge code.

USAGE

Merge operations in WordPerfect can become quite complex, as the program contains many sophisticated merge features. It is beyond the scope of this *Instant Reference* to present a complete tutorial in merge-printing with WordPerfect; instead, this guide briefly summarizes the rules for working with merge operations.

To perform a basic merge operation, such as a form letter, you usually create and use two separate files: a secondary file that contains all of the data to be substituted into each merged document (such as names and addresses), and a primary file (such as a letter) that indicates by special codes where each item from the secondary file is to be placed. If you do not need to save the variable data to use again, you can skip the process of creating the secondary file and instead enter each variable item from the keyboard as it is needed.

When the program performs the merge, it takes each record that you have specified from the secondary file and inserts its contents into the appropriate place in the primary file, creating a new merge file consisting of one filled-out standard document for each record.

The Primary File

Any primary file you use must indicate where the contents (fields) of the records in the secondary merge file are to be inserted. You do this by pressing Shift-F9, or choosing Merge Codes from the Tools menu, then selecting Field. You then enter the name or number of the field and press ↵. (In version 5.0, you do this by pressing Shift-F9, typing **F**, entering the number of the field (*n*), and pressing ↵. In Word-Perfect 5.1 the program displays *name* ~ at that point in your document. The variable *name* can be either a field name, such as customer address (note that you can use spaces), or a number. (In version 5.0 you can only use field numbers.) WordPerfect 5.1 displays the number of the current field at the bottom of the screen so that you can keep track of fields as you create your primary document. (See below for a description of how to use field names in version 5.1.)

Each time the program encounters a {FIELD}name~ in a primary file (or a field number in WordPerfect 5.0), it inserts the corresponding data from the *n*th (or *name*) field in the record that is current in the secondary merge file. For example, if the code were 1, WordPerfect would insert the contents of the first field in the current record. WordPerfect numbers fields sequentially beginning with 1 for the first data item.

If you are entering data from the keyboard instead of using a secondary file, enter a ^C merge code at each point in the document where you want to insert variable data. This instructs WordPerfect to pause for input.

Creating a Primary File

To create a primary merge file:

1. Begin a new document, such as a letter. Enter all of the text that is not to vary from merge document to merge document.

2. Indicate any places where you want information to be supplied from the secondary merge file by entering a name~ merge code. Do this by pressing Shift-F9 and choosing Field, or selecting Merge Codes from the Tools pull-down menu; enter a {KEYBOARD} merge code for input from the keyboard by choosing More and selecting {KEYBOARD}. In version 5.0, these codes are ^F and ^C, respectively. You cannot enter the correct codes by typing **{KEYBOARD}** or **{FIELD}name~**; you must enter them as described for your merge to take place successfully.

WordPerfect 5.0 places the field number inside a pair of carets (^) in the document. For instance, if you enter **2** after the Field prompt, it will appear as ^F2^ in the text when you press ↵. To delete a field from the primary file, you must delete the entire field designation, including the carets.

The Secondary File

The secondary merge file contains the data that will be inserted into the final merged documents. To prepare a secondary merge file, which is basically a database consisting of records and fields, you must follow a certain set of rules so that the program can accurately locate the data you want to use:

- Each item of data (field) must start on a separate line.

- Each line must be terminated by an {END FIELD} code (a ^R code in version 5.0), which indicates the end of a field. To insert this code, press F9.

- Each record must end with an {END RECORD} code (a ^E code in version 5.0), which indicates the end of a record. To insert this code, use the Merge Codes command and type **E**. WordPerfect will insert the code and a hard page break into the document.

- Each record must have the same number of fields, although some of them can be empty. This way, WordPerfect can always locate the correct data for, say, item 9, which would be in the ninth field. If records had variable numbers of fields, that data would not always be in the field with the same number.

- A field can contain more than one line of data. For example, you can use a field to contain an entire standard paragraph or clause in a contract and simply insert it each time it is needed.

- A field can contain several items of information, as long as you are willing to use those items as a unit. For example, a field may contain a complete name, such as *Rev. Evelyn Barker,* but you will not be able to break that name into smaller units in your final documents.

- In version 5.1, you can use field names instead of numbers. To do so, move to the beginning of the secondary document. Then choose More from the Merge Codes menu. From the menu that appears, choose {FIELD NAMES}name1~...nameN~. You will then be prompted to enter names for the field numbers you are using. For example, if the first field (field 1) holds the customer name, you may want to enter **customer name** at the "Field 1:" prompt. When you have assigned all the field names that you need, press F7 (Exit) to return to your secondary file. You will then see a new {FIELD NAMES} record listing all of the named fields you have set up, as the first record in the document. After you have assigned field names, you can reference the fields in the secondary file by name in your primary file instead of by number.

Creating a Secondary File

To create a secondary merge file:

1. Begin each information item (field) on its own line and terminate it with a Merge R code. (In version 5.0, this is an ^R code.) If you do not have information for a particular field, press F9 to enter a Merge R code to mark its position in the record.

2. Indicate where each record ends by entering a Merge E code on a separate line.

Performing a Merge

To perform a merge operation, press Ctrl-F9 (Merge/Sort) and select Merge or choose Merge from the Tools menu. You are then prompted to enter the names of the primary and secondary merge files to use. As soon as you enter the name of the file containing the secondary merge data you wish to use, WordPerfect begins the merge operation.

While the new file is being generated, you will see the message * *Merging* * displayed in the lower left corner of the screen. When the merge operation is completed, the cursor will be at the end of the file. Scroll through the file to make sure the correct data are in each field; then save the file.

Aborting a Merge   You can abort a merge operation at any time before it is finished by pressing F1 (Cancel). This causes WordPerfect to stop merging and to write any letters or forms that have been completed to the screen. (This is useful if you are using a large secondary file and you do not need to print documents for all the records.) To reexecute the merge operation, press F7 (Exit) and answer **N** to the prompt about saving the new document. You can then edit either the primary or secondary merge file and reissue the Merge command.

Merging to the Printer   WordPerfect doesn't automatically save a newly created merge file. When it completes a merge, it sends the merged file to the screen and simply holds it in RAM. If you have a large number of records in your secondary merge file, you may run out of RAM before WordPerfect generates all of the merged copies. If this occurs, the program stops the merge operation when no more memory is available and processes only part of your secondary merge file.

You can get around this limitation by using the technique WordPerfect calls *merging to the printer*. A special code, {PRINT} (^T in WordPerfect 5.0), instructs the program to send each document to the printer as it is completed and then clear its contents from RAM. *Note:* when you merge to the printer, you may need to insert additional codes that tell WordPerfect specifically which primary and secondary file to use for each merge, which records to use, and so forth (see **Merge Codes** below).

Merge Codes

WordPerfect offers many optional Merge codes that you can use to adapt the merge operation to special requirements. To insert a Merge code in a document, choose More from the Merge menu. To select a code, move the highlight cursor to it and press ⏎. You can also type the first letter of a code's name to move directly to it. In version 5.0, you press Shift-F9 (Merge Codes) and type the letter of the code.

Version 5.1 has changed the merge codes. In addition to the {FIELD}name~ (called ^F in version 5.0), {END FIELD} (^R in 5.0), and {END RECORD} (^E in 5.0), the following codes that have version 5.0 equivalents can be used in Word-Perfect 5.1:

{CHAIN MACRO}macroname~ —Replaces the version 5.0 ^G code; instructs the program to execute a macro when the merge terminates.

{DATE}—Replaces the version 5.0 ^D code; inserts the current date.

{INPUT}message~ —Replaces the version 5.0 ^Message ^O^C^O code combination; allows you to present a user-created message prompt or menu options on the screen. After the data is entered, the user presses F9 to resume the merge.

{KEYBOARD}—Replaces the version 5.0 ^C code; pauses the merge and allows you to enter data for a field directly from the keyboard.

{MRG CMND}codes{MRG CMND}—Replaces the version 5.0 ^V code; allows you to insert merge codes into the document currently being created. This command is quite useful for setting up a complex merge operation that adds records that you can transfer to an existing secondary merge document. Thus, you can essentially automate the procedure of adding records to any of your secondary merge files.

{NEST PRIMARY}filename~ —Replaces the version 5.0 ^P code; designates the primary file to be used so that you can switch to a different primary file during a merge.

{NEXT RECORD}—Replaces the version 5.0 ^N code that told the program to go to the next record. Insert this code by choosing Next Record from the Merge Codes menu.

{PAGE OFF}—Replaces the version 5.0 ^N^P^P combination; tells the program not to place a hard page break after each primary file. Insert this code by choosing Page Off from the Merge Codes menu.

{PRINT}—Replaces the version 5.0 ^T code; sends text that has been merged up to the location of that code to the printer.

{PROMPT}message~ —Replaces the version 5.0 ^O code; allows you to present a message on the screen.

{QUIT}—Replaces the version 5.0 ^Q code; terminates a merge operation.

{REWRITE}—Replaces the version 5.0 ^U code; rewrites the screen, causing the merge document currently being generated to be displayed on the screen.

{SUBST SECONDARY}filename~ —Replaces the version 5.0 ^S code; allows you to specify a secondary file to be switched to during a merge.

In addition to these codes, version 5.1 allows you to use many other sophisticated merge commands that control merge operations. For example, you can chain primary and secondary files so that when one merge finishes, another automatically begins, and nest merge files so WordPerfect will switch to them during a merge. In addition, special merge commands allow you to direct WordPerfect to specific fields during a merge. These and other merge commands are described in detail in your reference manual.

You can use merge documents created in version 5.0 with version 5.1, or you can update the codes to the new system by selecting Ctrl-F9 then Convert old Merge Codes.

Merging Delimited Files

You may often want to use WordPerfect's Merge feature with secondary files such as a database of names and addresses that was created in a database program. In database files used for mail merge operations, fields and records are arranged by using *delimiters,* which are special characters that indicate the ends of fields and records. Some programs use beginning and end delimiters; some use only end delimiters. If you are setting up a merge with one of these ASCII delimited files, you can tell WordPerfect 5.1 what the delimiter characters are as you begin the merge. When you are prompted for the name of the secondary file to use, press Ctrl-F5 (Text In/Out) and enter the name of that file. You can then indicate which field and record delimiters that the DOS text delimited file uses. (If you use the same type of file often for merges, you can use the Setup menu to indicate what the delimiters are.) You will see that WordPerfect has set the default end-field delimiter to be a comma and the default end-record delimiter to be a carriage return. If these are not the characters used by your database program, you can change them to the characters used in the files you are working with. WordPerfect will then place the {END FIELD} and {END RECORD} codes at the proper locations when you merge the files.

Mouse (Version 5.1)

Version 5.1 allows you to use a mouse to highlight text, move the cursor, and select commands and functions without using the keyboard.

To use a mouse with WordPerfect 5.1, you must first install it according to the documentation that came with your mouse. Then use the Setup menu to tell the program what kind of mouse you are using, which port it is attached to, and so forth.

You can use a mouse to select features and commands as well as using the keyboard, or you can use a combination of the two. To display the pull-down menu, click the right mouse button (note: if you are using the mouse as a left-handed mouse, keep in mind that your mouse buttons are reversed). To remove the pull-down menu display, click the right button again (or press F7 or the Space bar).

When a pull-down menu is displayed, you can move the mouse pointer to an item and click the left mouse button to select it, or you can press and hold the left mouse button down and drag the pointer to an item, releasing the left mouse button to select it. When a regular menu is displayed, you can click on an item to select it or click with the right button to remove the menu from the screen. The right mouse button works like the F7 (Exit) key, but it will not exit you from WordPerfect.

Keep in mind that the mouse pointer is not the same as the cursor; the cursor indicates the current entry point in your document. When you move the mouse pointer to a location on the screen and click the left mouse button, you move the cursor to that location.

You can also click on prompts to select the highlighted command that the prompt is displaying, such as Yes (No). To accept the default response, double-click the left mouse button; it works the same as pressing ⏎.

When WordPerfect is displaying a list of items, such as when you are in the List Files screen, the Select Printer screen, or the Base Font screen, you can double-click on an item to select it. In List Files, double-clicking lets you look at the contents of a file or directory.

To use the mouse with the Search function, select Search, enter the pattern to search for, and press the right mouse button.

If you need to see parts of your document that are not visible on the screen, you can use the mouse to scroll to them. Press the right mouse button and then drag the mouse to the edge of the screen in the direction you want to scroll (right, left, up, or down). To stop scrolling, release the mouse button. To block text and scroll at the same time, use the left mouse button.

To cancel a command or restore a deletion with a two-button mouse, press either mouse button and hold it down. Click the other button and release both. On a three-button mouse, the middle button works like the F1 (Cancel) key. Most commands can be cancelled by pressing the right mouse button.

NOTE

Do not use the mouse to position the cursor when you are defining a macro; use the arrow keys instead.

SEE ALSO

Pull-Down Menus.

Move/Rename File

Allows you to move a file to a new directory or rename it.

SEQUENCE OF STEPS

F5 (List Files) ↵ *or* ⌨ ➠ **File** pull-down *then* **List Files** ↵

➠ *[highlight file to move or rename]*

➡ **M**ove/Rename

➡ *<new path name to move and/or file name to rename>* ⏎

USAGE

The Move/Rename option on the List Files menu allows you to rename files in the directory listing or to move them to a new disk or directory on your hard disk. When you select this option after highlighting the file to be moved or renamed (as indicated in the step sequence), you receive the prompt *New name:* followed by the current file name. To rename it, edit or retype the file name. To move it to a new directory, edit the path name and leave the file name as is. To move a file and rename it simultaneously, edit both the path name and the file name. After making these changes, press ⏎. If you renamed the document, the new name will appear in the directory listing after you press ⏎. If you moved the document, its name will no longer appear in the listing (you must change directories to see it).

You can use the Move/Rename option to relocate multiple files in one operation. Mark all of the files to be moved with an asterisk (*) by moving the cursor highlight to each one and typing * (you can mark all of the files in the List Files listing at one time by pressing Alt-F5). After marking the files to be moved, select the Move/Rename option, enter the name of the drive/directory that they are to be moved to, and press ⏎.

SEE ALSO

Copying Files.

Name Search

Moves the highlight cursor directly to the file or font name whose initial characters match those you enter.

SEQUENCE OF STEPS

To locate a file or font from a list on a menu screen:

N Name Search *or* **F2** (→Search)

➠ *<character(s) to search for>*

➠ *↵ or arrow key to exit*

USAGE

The Name Search feature positions the highlight cursor on the first file or font whose name matches the character or characters entered. It enables you to locate and select a particular file or font in a long listing with just a few keystrokes.

With version 5.0 you must press F2 (Search) to initiate a Name Search on some screens. In version 5.1 you can use the Name Search feature whenever a list is displayed, such as a list of fonts, macro commands, or merge commands, by typing **N**. As you type your first character, the highlight cursor jumps to a file or font name that matches that character. As you continue to type characters, the search narrows, moving the highlight to the first file whose name begins with the matching characters. To exit a name search, press ↵ or one of the four arrow keys.

SEE ALSO

Find.

Outlining

Creates an outline by automatically numbering paragraphs
as you enter each level.

SEQUENCE OF STEPS

To create an outline:

> **Shift-F5** (Date/Outline) *or* ▭ **T**ools pull-down
>
> ⇒ **O**utline
>
> ⇒ **O**n (*to turn on*)
>
> ⇒ ↵ *<text for level 1>* ↵
>
> ⇒ **Tab** *<text for next level>* ↵

To define the outlining style:

> **Shift-F5** (Date/Outline) *or* ▭ **T**ools pull-down
>
> ⇒ **D**efine
>
> ⇒ **S**tarting Paragraph Number (in legal style);
> **P**aragraph; **O**utline; **L**egal (1.1.1); **B**ullets;
> **U**ser-Defined; **E**nter Inserts New Paragraph
> Number **Y**; **A**utomatically Adjust to Current Level **Y**;
> Outline Style **N**ame
>
> ⇒ **F7** (Exit)

Note: In version 5.0, the last three options under the Define
menu are omitted.

To create an outline style (version 5.1):

> **Shift-F5** (Date/Outline) *or* ▭ **T**ools
>
> ⇒ **D**efine
>
> ⇒ Outline Style **N**ame
>
> ⇒ **C**reate

➠ **N**ame; **D**escription; **T**ype; **E**nter; **C**odes

➠ **F7** (Exit)

USAGE

After you have turned on Outline mode, each time you enter characters or a space and then press ↵, a new outline number is generated in your text. To generate a number at a lower level, press the Tab key after pressing ↵. In version 5.1 you can specify whether you want pressing ↵ to generate a new outline number (it is preset to do so) and whether that number should be at a fixed level (see below).

While you are in Outline mode, the prompt *Outline* appears in the lower-left corner of your screen. In version 5.0, to turn off Outline mode, press Shift-F5 (Date/Outline) and select the Outline option again. In version 5.1, choose On or Off to turn outlining on and off. Outline mode must be on (the Outline message must be visible on the screen) in order for automatic outline numbering to work.

With the default settings in version 5.1, to indent text without entering an outline number or letter when you are in Outline mode, press the space bar before you press the Tab key. You can also use →Indent (F4) or →Indent← (Shift-F4) to indent text without inserting outline numbers.

Working with Outline Families

Version 5.1 also allows you to work with associated entries in an outline, which it calls an outline family. An outline family includes the level of the line that contains the cursor as well as subordinate outline entries. For example, if your cursor were on the line containing item II in an outline and there were subordinate entries below it (items A and B), those items plus all of their subordinate entries (II.A.1, II.A.2, II.B.1, II.B.2, and so forth) would be considered an outline family. You can move, copy, and delete outline families, which allows you to restructure and edit your outlines quickly. Moving, copying, and deleting outline families works similarly to block moving and copying: when the cursor is located on the line where you want to begin moving, copying, or deleting that item plus all the successive related items below it, press Shift-F5 (Date/Outline) or choose Outline from the Tools menu; then choose one of the family options—Move Family, Copy Family, or Delete Family. Once you have deleted a family, you can restore it immediately at another location by pressing Shift-F10 (Retrieve) and pressing ↵.

Defining the Style of Paragraph/Outline Numbering

WordPerfect's default outlining style follows the system I., A., 1., a., (1), (a), i), a). You can use more than these eight levels; the eighth-level definition is used for the levels after the eighth, and each level is indented one additional tab stop. There are also three other numbering styles built into the program: paragraph style, which uses the system 1., a., i., (1), (a), (i), 1), a); legal style, which numbers each paragraph and level sequentially as 1, 1.1, 1.1.1, and so forth, and bullet style, which uses a system of symbols that not all printers can produce. You can also change the system of numbering and punctuation by using the User-Defined option and specifying a custom style.

Version 5.1 lets you specify whether it should automatically adjust the outline to the current level. It is preset to Yes, but if you want the program to always use a first-level number, such as I., II., III., and so forth, change this setting to No. You can also change whether pressing ↵ inserts a new level or simply a hard return when you are in Outline mode.

Creating Styles for Outlines

In version 5.1, you can create styles for your outlines by using the Outline Style Name option. It allows you to create a style for each numbering level and to maintain a library of those styles that you can choose from at any time. Creating an outline style (see the step sequence above) is similar to creating a style in the Style menu (Alt-F8): Choose Create; move the cursor to the level you are creating a new style for; then enter the information about it, such as its name and description, type (open or paired), and so forth. If the style is a paired style, you can choose whether pressing ↵ turns it off or off and on again by using the Enter option. At the Codes option, you can specify text and text attributes, such as bold and italic, and sizes, such as Small or Large, or specify a different font for your outline numbers. For information about how to create and work with styles, see **Styles** in this reference.

SEE ALSO

Line Numbering; Paragraph Numbering.

Overstrike

Prints two (or more) characters or fonts in the same position.

SEQUENCE OF STEPS

Shift-F8 (Format) *or* ⌐ **L**ayout pull-down

⇒ **O**ther

⇒ **O**verstrike

⇒ **C**reate; **E**dit

⇒ *[enter or edit characters or fonts]* ↵

⇒ **F7** (Exit)

USAGE

You can use the Overstrike feature to create composite characters, such as foreign-language characters that use accent marks or special math/science symbols. This is helpful if your printer is unable to print characters in WordPerfect's Character sets created with the Compose feature (see **Compose**). You can also use Overstrike to have your printer combine attributes available from the Font, Size, or Color menus that appear when you press Ctrl-F8 (Font).

When you enter the characters and/or font attributes for Overstrike (as shown in the step sequence), you see all of the characters and attribute codes as you enter them. When you press ↵ and F7 (Exit) to return to the editing screen, you see there only the last character entered. WordPerfect prints all of the characters and attributes included in the Overstrike definition in the same position in the document.

To edit a composite character created with Overstrike, bring up the Reveal Codes screen with Alt-F3, position the cursor immediately following the [Ovrstk:] code, and select the Edit option as indicated in the step sequence. Enter the new characters and/or attributes, press ↵, and then press F7 (Exit) to return to the editing screen.

To delete a composite character created with Overstrike, locate and delete the appropriate [Ovrstk:] code in the Reveal Codes screen.

SEE ALSO

Compose.

Page Break, Soft and Hard

Divides pages automatically according to the top and bottom margins, the size of the page, and the printer selected (soft page break), or ends a page at the discretion of the user (hard page break).

SEQUENCE OF STEPS

To enter a hard page break in the document:

Ctrl-↵ *or* ⌨ Layout pull-down *then* Align *then*
Hard **P**age

USAGE

WordPerfect automatically adjusts soft page breaks as you edit your document. They are displayed as a line of dashes on the screen. To change the placement of a soft page break, change the top and bottom margins, or delete lines of text on the page.

You can insert hard page breaks by pressing Ctrl-↵ at the point where you want a page break to occur or by selecting Tools, Align, and Hard Page from the pull-down menus. For example, you might want to end a short page at the end of one section of a report so that the next main topic would begin a new page. Hard page breaks are represented by a line of equal signs across the screen.

Hard page breaks are also used to indicate the end of a column when you are using WordPerfect's Columns feature.

To delete a hard page break, position the cursor next to the line of equal signs that represents it and press Backspace or Delete, or locate and delete the [HPg] code in the Reveal Codes screen.

SEE ALSO

Columns, Text (Newspaper and Parallel); Conditional End of Page; Widow/Orphan Protection.

Page Numbering

Adds page numbers that are automatically updated when you make editing changes that affect pagination.

SEQUENCE OF STEPS

To turn on and off page numbering:

Shift-F8 (Format) *or* 🖱 **Layout** pull-down

⮕ **Page**

▦▶ Page **N**umbering

▦▶ **N**ew Page Number; Page Numbering **S**tyle; **I**nsert Page Number; Page Number **P**osition

Note: In version 5.0, your options are somewhat different. To turn off page numbering, choose No Page Numbers after selecting Page Numbering. To specify a new starting page number, choose New Page Number from the Page Format menu.

USAGE

WordPerfect is preset for no page numbering, but you can turn on page numbering at any point in your document by using the Page Numbering option on the Page Format menu as indicated in the step sequence. When you select Page Numbering, you will see a menu from which you can indicate whether numbering should begin with a number other than 1; set a page numbering style that can (in version 5.1) include text (such as *Final Report: Page 4* or *Chapter 12, Page 10*); insert (in version 5.1) the current page number somewhere else on the page (such as in a header or footnote); and specify the position where the page number will appear on the page. You can enter a new page number or change the numbering system from Arabic (1, 2, 3) to upper- or lowercase Roman (I, II, III; i, ii, iii) by using the New Page Number option and typing in the new number. If you want page numbers to include text, choose Page Number Style and enter the text as you want it to appear, up to 30 characters. Include any size and appearance changes in the font. Type (Ctrl-B) where you want the page number—for example, **Page ^B**. WordPerfect will insert the Ctrl-B for you at the last cursor position if you leave it out.

To specify that the page number style appear somewhere else in your document, such as in a header or within text, move the cursor to the location where you want the page number style to appear and then choose Insert Page Number. If your page number style is simply ^B (that is, if there is no text as part of the page number style), you can simply press Ctrl-B where you want the page number to appear (see below).

When you choose Page Number Position, you will see a menu that presents eight different choices for page number positions on every page or on alternating pages. (If you are using version 5.0, you will see this menu as soon as you choose the Page Numbering option on the Page menu.) Choose options 1–3 and 5–7 for page numbers to appear in the same place on every page. Options 4 and 8 will insert page numbers in different locations on alternating left and right pages. Option 9 turns off page numbering. If you are not specifying text to be used with page numbers, choosing Page Number Position is all you need to do to turn on Arabic page numbering.

When you return to your document by pressing F7 (Exit), you will not see page numbers on the screen, but they will appear when the document is printed. You can use the View Document feature to view page numbers in position on the screen.

You can also use page numbering by inserting the code ^B in your document. For example, if you want your headers or footers to contain page numbers, enter a ^B (Ctrl-B) at the position where you want the page number to occur. To specify the position of page numbers in headers and footers, press Alt-F6 (Flush Right) or Shift-F6 (Center) before you enter the ^B. If you are using both the Page Numbering feature and the Headers or Footers feature, be sure to insert an extra blank line at the beginning of the header or at the end of the footer so that WordPerfect will have a line on which to print the page number by itself; otherwise the page number will overprint the last line of the header or footer.

When you begin numbering with a new page number, you will see the change reflected on the status line. Be sure to move the cursor to the beginning of the page where you want numbering to start when you use either the Page Numbering or New Page Number option.

To suppress page numbering on any given page, use the Suppress option of the Page Format menu. To turn off page numbering, use the No Page Numbers option on the Page Numbering Position menu.

SEE ALSO

Headers and Footers; Suppress Page Format.

Paper Size/ Type

Instructs WordPerfect to use a new page size or form definition in printing.

SEQUENCE OF STEPS

Shift-F8 (Format) *or* **L**ayout pull-down

➠ **P**age

➠ Paper **S**ize/ Type *<highlight paper type>*

➠ **S**elect

➠ **F7** (Exit)

To set up a new paper size and type:

Shift-F8 (Format) *or* ⌨ **L**ayout pull-down

➠ **P**age

➠ Paper **S**ize/ Type

➠ **A**dd

➠ *<choose paper type>* Paper **S**ize; Paper **T**ype; **F**ont
Type; **P**rompt to Load; **L**ocation; **D**ouble Sided
Printing; **B**inding Edge; **L**abels; **T**ext Adjustment

➠ **F7 F7 F7** (Exit)

WordPerfect is preset to use 8 1/2 × 11-inch paper, but you
can change to a different size and type of paper by using the
Paper Size/Type option on the Page Format menu. In version 5.1 this feature is a streamlined version of the Forms feature of version 5.0; if you are using version 5.0, see **Forms** in
this reference.

When you choose the Paper Size/Type option, you will
see a list of the paper sizes and types that have been defined
for the printer that is currently selected. You can select one of
these or select Add to create a new paper size and type, or if

one that is close to what you want is listed, you can copy it and edit it.

If you choose Add, you will be asked to choose a paper type from a menu of several standard types, or choose Other and enter the name of the form you are using. After you specify the paper type, you can specify a size. In addition, you can choose Font Type to specify whether the font is Landscape (printed sideways on the page) or Portrait (printed in the normal orientation). Choose Prompt to Load if you want WordPerfect to prompt you to load a special paper into your printer when you print a document using this paper size and type. The Location option allows you to specify whether the paper will be sheet-fed from a bin, manually fed, or continuous form. Choose Double Sided Binding if you are printing on both sides of the paper and planning to bind the document. The Binding Edge option allows you to specify whether the document should be printed so that it can be bound at the top or on the left side. The Labels option is used when you are printing mailing labels; see **Labels** in this reference. The final option, Text Adjustment, allows you to adjust the placement of the text on the page if your document is not printing properly.

SEE ALSO

Forms (version 5.0); Labels (version 5.1).

Paragraph Numbering

Automatically numbers paragraphs as you enter them.

SEQUENCE OF STEPS

To number a paragraph:

Shift-F5 (Date/Outline) *or* ⌨ **Tools** pull-down

➡ **Para Num**

⇒ Paragraph Level (Press Enter for Automatic): *<level
number, 1–8>* or ↵ *or* the right ⌐ button

⇒ *<text of paragraph>* ↵

USAGE

To number paragraphs automatically, press Shift-F5 (Date/
Outline), or use the Tools pull-down menu, and select the Paragraph Number option. You will be prompted to enter a paragraph level number. You can simply press ↵ or the right
mouse button for automatic paragraph numbering. When you
press ↵, WordPerfect will insert a paragraph number. Each
level of numbering is associated with a tab stop. To enter
progressively lower levels of paragraph numbers, press the Tab
key until you reach the level you want. Then press Shift-F5,
select the Paragraph Number option, and press ↵.

You can also use *fixed numbering,* in which a particular
numbering style will be inserted no matter which tab stop
you are on. To use fixed numbering, enter the level (1–8) you
want to use when you are prompted for the paragraph level.

Defining the
Style of Paragraph Numbering

WordPerfect is preset to use the outline style of numbering (I.,
A., 1., etc.). It also has a built-in paragraph numbering style
(1., a., i., etc.) and a legal numbering style (1., 1.1., 1.1.1., etc.).
To select the paragraph or legal numbering style:

1. Press Shift-F5 (Date/Outline) and select the Define option, or choose Define from the Tools menu.

2. When the Paragraph Numbering Definition screen appears, select a numbering style from the options on the
   screen or create a style of your own by entering any
   combination of styles and symbols from the choices
   available. See **Outlining** for a discussion of the options.

| SEE ALSO |

Line Numbering; Outlining; Styles.

Print Color

Allows you to select the color of the text (when printed), if you have a color printer.

| SEQUENCE OF STEPS |

Ctrl-F8 (Font) *or* ▭ F**o**nt pull-down

➠ Print **C**olor

➠ **B**lack; **W**hite; **R**ed; **G**reen; **B**lue; **Y**ellow; **M**agenta; **C**yan; **O**range; **G**ray; **B**rown; **O**ther

➠ **F7** (Exit)

| USAGE |

If you have a color printer, you can use the Print Color option on the Font menu to select different colors of text for the printed page. For example, you might want to print cover sheets for each section of a document or chapter of a book in a different color, or you might want to highlight a specific section of text by printing it in color.

To return to black printing after having selected a different color, select the Black option from the list of color options and press Exit (F7).

To specify a custom color, you can select the Other option and enter an intensity percentage for red, green, and blue.

The Print Color option controls the color the document is printed in, not the color of the characters on the screen.

Print Job, Cancel

Allows you to remove a print job from the print queue.

Shift-F7 (Print) *or* ⌨ File pull-down *then* **Print**

➡ **C**ontrol Printer

➡ Cancel Jobs)

➡ *<job number> or* * **Y** (to cancel all jobs)

➡ **F7** (Exit)

Selecting the Cancel Job(s) option while the Control Printer screen is displayed allows you to cancel a specific print job in the print queue. When WordPerfect prompts you for the job to cancel, enter the job number of the document that is being printed or the job you want to cancel and press ↵. You may need to press ↵ again if your printer does not respond. If you are using a large printer buffer, several seconds may elapse before your printer stops printing what has already been sent to it. To cancel all print jobs, enter an asterisk (*), answer **Y** to the prompt *Cancel all print jobs?*, and press ↵.

If you cancel all print jobs, you may get a message informing you that you will need to initialize your printer before you can continue printing. You may also need to adjust the paper in the printer before you resume printing.

Printer Control; Print Job, Display; Print Job, Rush.

Print Job, Display

Allows you to see the remaining print jobs in the queue beyond those displayed on the Control Printer screen.

SEQUENCE OF STEPS

Shift-F7 (Print) *or* ⌐⃗ **File** pull-down *then* **P**rint

➠ **Control Printer**

➠ **D**isplay Job(s)

➠ **F7** (Exit)

USAGE

Each time you send a document to the printer, WordPerfect assigns it a job number. The first three print jobs are listed on the Control Printer screen; an *Additional Jobs Not Shown* message indicates that there are additional print jobs that are not listed on the Control Printer screen. You can use the Display Jobs option to see all of the current print jobs, if there are more than three.

Viewing the print job numbers is useful if you are selecting a print job to cancel or bring to the head of the print queue.

SEE ALSO

Print Job, Cancel; Print Job, Rush.

Print Job, Rush

Allows you to select a print job to be sent to the top of the queue.

SEQUENCE OF STEPS

Shift-F7 (Print) ⌐▷ *or* **F**ile pull-down *then* **P**rint

➡ **C**ontrol Printer

➡ **R**ush Job

➡ *<job number>*

➡ **F7** (Exit)

USAGE

To move a print job to the head of the queue, select the Rush Job option from the Control Printer screen. WordPerfect will prompt you for the number of the job to rush. Enter the job number and press ↵. If you answer **Y** to the Interrupt prompt, WordPerfect will immediately print your rush job and then resume printing the job it was working on. If you answer **N**, it will print the rush job as soon as the current job is finished.

If the job you want to rush is a new print job that you haven't yet sent to the printer, first send it to the printer in the normal way; then select the Rush Job option and enter the job number for that job.

SEE ALSO

Print Job, Cancel; Print Job, Display.

Print Multiple Pages

Allows you to print selected pages from the document on the screen (version 5.1).

SEQUENCE OF STEPS

Shift-F7 (Print) *or* ⌐ᗈ **F**ile pull-down *then* **P**rint

➠ **M**ultiple pages

➠ *<enter page range>* ↵

USAGE

WordPerfect 5.1 allows you to print selected pages from the document that is on the screen, even if it has not been saved. When you use this option, enter the page pattern as **x-y** to print pages x through y; **x, y** or **x y** to print pages x and y; **x-** to print page x to the end of the document; and **-y** to print from the top of the document to page y. (See **Printing** for additional examples of page patterns.)

If you need several copies of a particular group of pages, choose Number of Copies (option N) and enter the number of copies of the selected pages you want.

Normally WordPerfect will generate the extra copies, but it can save time when you are using downloadable fonts or printing graphics if you specify that your printer handle multiple copies.

Print Options

Allows you to specify the settings to be used for binding, print quality, multiple copies, and so forth.

SEQUENCE OF STEPS

To change print options for the current document:

Shift-F7 (Print) *or* 🖰 **F**ile pull-down *then* **P**rint

⮕ **S**elect Printer; **B**inding Offset; **N**umber of Copies; **M**ultiple Copies Generated by; **G**raphics Quality; **T**ext Quality

⮕ **F7** (Exit)

USAGE

To change print options for the document you are working with, use the Print screen (Shift-F7). The options in the lower half of the screen are the printing options that can be changed for each individual print job. Version 5.1 has added the Multiple Copies Generated by option, which allows you to specify whether WordPerfect or your printer generates multiple copies.

Many laser printers can print several copies of specified pages. Normally WordPerfect will generate the extra copies, but if you are using downloadable fonts or printing graphics, you may find it faster to specify that your printer generate the multiple copies by choosing the Multiple Copies Generated By option and selecting Printer instead of WordPerfect. If you are using WordPerfect on a network, your network may also have this capability.

SEE ALSO

Binding Offset; Print Multiple Pages; Print Quality; Redline/Strikeout.

Print Quality

Allows you to specify the print quality to be used for text and graphics as well as to print graphics separate from the text in your document.

SEQUENCE OF STEPS

To change the graphics print quality or to print text only:

   Shift-F7 (Print) *or* ⌐🖰 **F**ile pull-down *then* **P**rint

   ➠ **G**raphics Quality

   ➠ **D**o **N**ot Print; **D**raft; **M**edium; **H**igh

To change the text print quality or to print graphics only:

   Shift-F7 (Print) ⌐🖰 *or* **F**ile pull-down *then* **P**rint

   ➠ **T**ext Quality

   ➠ **D**o **N**ot Print; **D**raft; **M**edium; **H**igh

USAGE

The Graphics Quality and Text Quality options on the Print menu control the quality of document printing (draft, medium, and high) for the text and graphic images in your document. You can use these options to prepare rough drafts of documents and to print graphics, which take longer to print, separately from document text. You can select a different print quality for both text and graphics. WordPerfect prints color graphics in black and white, using shading for the color areas.

Your printer may be capable of printing both text and graphics, but not at the same time. If this is the case, you can use the Do Not Print option after selecting the Graphics Quality option to print just the text. Then reinsert the paper in the printer and print just the graphics by selecting the Do Not Print option after choosing the Text Quality option.

Print Quality settings apply to every print job until you change them again or quit WordPerfect.

Note: If your graphics do not print completely on a laser printer, you may need additional memory. Graphic images take up a large amount of memory.

Printer Command

Inserts special printer formatting commands that are sent to the printer when your document is printed.

SEQUENCE OF STEPS

Shift-F8 (Format) *or* ⌧ **L**ayout pull-down

➠ **O**ther

➠ **P**rinter Functions

➠ **P**rinter Command

➠ **C**ommand; **F**ilename

➠ *<printer command codes or filename>* ↵

➠ **F7** (Exit)

USAGE

You can use the Other option on the Format menu (Shift-F8) or the Layout pull-down menu to display the Printer Functions menu and insert special printer codes that turn on special effects your printer is capable of producing. However, WordPerfect can provide most common printer features directly.

To use special printing effects that WordPerfect does not support directly, you must insert a code that WordPerfect sends to your printer to tell it what to do. These codes are specific to each printer, and you must consult your printer manual for a list of the codes used.

To issue a printer command, enter the ASCII code for the printing effect you want. You cannot enter ASCII codes less than 32 or greater than 126 directly from the keyboard, but instead must enter their decimal equivalents, enclosed in angle brackets. ASCII codes are case-sensitive: Uppercase *A* (ASCII code 065) is not the same as lowercase *a* (ASCII code 097), for example.

For example, to enter the sequence *Esc* # for your printer, you do not enter the letters *esc* or press the Esc key. Instead, you enter the decimal ASCII equivalent of Esc, 27, enclosed in angle brackets and followed by the # symbol. To do this, you select the Command option as indicated in the step sequence and then enter **<27>#** after the Cmnd: prompt. The format code entered for this printer command (visible only when you use Reveal Codes) will appear as *[Cmnd:<27>#]*. You will not see printer commands on the screen, but they will be sent to the printer when you print your document.

Printer Control

Allows you to examine and make modifications to the jobs in the printer queue, as well as to start and stop printing.

SEQUENCE OF STEPS

Shift-F7 (Print) *or* ⌒ᗺ **File** pull-down *then* **P**rint

➠ **C**ontrol Printer

➠ **C**ancel Job(s); **R**ush Job; **D**isplay Jobs; **G**o (start printer); **S**top

USAGE

To control the printing process as it is going on, select the Control Printer option from the Print menu. Doing this brings you to the Control Printer screen, where you may cancel specific print jobs, start a rush print job, display print jobs, restart the printer after it has been stopped, or stop the printer without canceling print jobs.

After you have temporarily stopped the printer, you can start it again by using the Go option on this menu.

| SEE ALSO |

Print Job, Cancel; Print Job, Display; Print Job, Rush; Printing, Stop.

Printer, Select

Allows you to install a printer, edit a printer definition, or select a new printer.

| SEQUENCE OF STEPS |

To select a new printer:

Shift-F7 (Printer) *or* ⌐⊟ **F**ile pull-down *then* **P**rint

➠ **S**elect Printer

➠ *[highlight the name of the printer]*

➠ **S**elect

➠ **F7** (Exit)

To install a new printer:

Shift-F7 (Printer) *or* ⌐⊟ **F**ile pull-down *then* **P**rint

➠ **S**elect Printer

➠ **A**dditional Printers

➠ **S**elect; **O**ther Disk; **H**elp; **L**ist Printer Files; **N**ame Search

➠ **F7** (Exit)

To edit a printer definition:

Shift-F7 (Print) *or* ⌐⊟ **F**ile *then* **P**rint

➠ **S**elect Printer

➠ *[highlight of the name of the printer]*

➠ **E**dit

➠ **N**ame; **P**ort; **S**heet Feeder; **C**artridges and Fonts; **I**nitial Base Font; Path for **D**ownloadable Fonts and Printer Command Files

➠ **F7** (Exit)

Note: The Forms option in version 5.0 is no longer on the Edit Printer menu. In version 5.1, these settings are on the Paper Size/Type option of the Page Format menu (see **Paper Size/Type**). If you are using version 5.0. this option indicates the location of the paper sizes and types you intend to use with the printer (see **Forms**).

USAGE

WordPerfect saves the printer selection you have made for each document with that document. In version 5.1, you can use the Initial Settings submenu of the Setup menu to specify that retrieved documents be formatted for the printer that is currently selected.

To select a printer for the document, select Print and choose the Select Printer option. The program will display a list of printers that you have installed, and an asterisk (*) will appear next to the name of the currently selected printer. You can move the highlighting to the printer you want to use and press ⏎ to select it, or select an option from the following menu:

1 Select; **2 A**dditional Printers; **3 E**dit; **4 C**opy; **5 D**elete; **6 H**elp; **7 U**pdate:1

Version 5.1 has added the last option, Update, to make updating your printer driver quicker. From time to time Wordperfect issues new printer drivers with its interim releases. (To see the date of your release, press F3 from the Editing screen and check the upper-right corner.) If you get a new release of WordPerfect, you may want to update your printer driver. To use this option, first delete the old .ALL files from your directory; then copy the new .ALL files from your new WordPerfect disk into your directory. You can then choose this option to update your printer driver.

Installing a New Printer

If the printer you want to use is not displayed, use the Additional Printers option to install it. If the program cannot find the additional printer files, use the Other Disk option to direct it to the drive or directory containing the additional printer files. The printer drivers are on Printer disks 1 through 4. The program will display a list of the printer drivers on each disk. When you see the printer you want to install, move the cursor to highlight its name; then press ↵. The Name Search option allows you to search for a specific printer's name. When you select a printer, WordPerfect will display the printer definition file (with the .PRS extension) used by this printer. Press ↵ again to have the program copy this file (see **Establishing a Printer Definition**).

Viewing Installed Printers

As you are selecting new printers, you may want to review the list of printers you have already installed. The List Printer Files option on the Additional Printers submenu allows you to view a list of the installed printers. WordPerfect keeps information about printer drivers in files with an .ALL extension. Once a printer file is created, its definition is kept in a file with a .PRS extension, which is what you see listed on this screen.

Establishing a Printer Definition

After you have selected a new printer, you will see the Printer Helps and Hints screen, which contains information about the specific printer you are installing. Press F7 (Exit) to go to the next menu, where you can change the printer's name, specify which port it is connected to, select a sheet feeder, select forms, specify cartridges and fonts, set the default font that the printer is to use, and specify a path for downloadable fonts and printer command files.

Establishing Printer Settings

The Name option allows you to change the name that appears on the Select Printer: Edit menu. You can enter up to 36 characters for a new name.

The Port option is used to indicate the port your printer is connected to. The default setting is LPT1, the first parallel printer port. If the printer whose definition you just chose is connected to another parallel port, select Port. You will see a menu listing LPT ports 1 through 3 and COM ports 1 through 4. If your printer is connected to a different port, select the Other option and specify the device name.

When defining a printer that uses a serial port, you will see a screen indicating the baud rate, parity, number of stop bits, character length, and type of hardware handshaking (XON/XOFF) that your printer normally uses. If you are using different settings, select them and change them. All of the settings possible for your printer should be in your printer manual.

Use the Sheet Feeder option if you are using a sheet feeder to feed paper into your printer. Select the sheet feeder that you are using; then choose the Select option. A Helps and Hints screen will appear after you have selected the sheet feeder, and the sheet feeder definition will be copied into the .PRS file that is being created for your printer definition.

The Cartridges and Fonts option indicates the fonts and cartridges you plan to use with the printer (see **Cartridges and Fonts**). The Initial Base Font option indicates the current default font to be used with that printer. The font selected as the initial font will be used each time you start a new document. To override it, you can use the Initial Font option on the Document Format menu or change it through the Base Font option (see **Base Font**). The last option is used to indicate the path name for the subdirectory in which you are storing downloadable fonts or printer command files (see **Cartridges and Fonts** and **Printer Command**).

Editing Printer Definitions

The Edit and Copy options of the Print: Select Printer menu allow you to copy and then modify an existing printer definition. For example, you might want to set up the same physical printer with two different definitions under different names. The first definition might specify a different default font or sheet feeder from the second definition, and you could quickly choose either "printer" by selecting its name from the list of installed printers.

You can also use the Select Printer option to delete a printer from the list of installed printers by choosing the Delete option. To get additional help about the specific printers you have installed, use the Help option. To get help with a sheet feeder, press Shift-F3 (Switch) when you are viewing the Printer Help screen.

SEE ALSO

Base Font; Cartridges and Fonts; Forms (version 5.0); Paper Size/Type; Printing.

Printing

Prints all or part of a document using the selected printer.

SEQUENCE OF STEPS

To print the current page, a range of pages, or the entire document on your editing screen:

Shift-F7 (Print) *or* ꝏ **F**ile *then* **P**rint

➠ **F**ull Document; **P**age; **M**ultiple Pages *<page range>*

Note: In version 5.0, the Multiple Pages option is omitted.

To print a document on disk:

> **Shift-F7** (Print) *or* ⌐▭ **F**ile *then* **P**rint
>
> ➠ **D**ocument on Disk
>
> ➠ Document name: *<file name>* ↵
>
> ➠ Page(s): ↵ *(to print all)* or *<range or selected page numbers>* ↵

To print a document on disk from the List Files menu:

> **F5** (List Files) ↵
>
> ➠ *[highlight name of file to be printed]*
>
> ➠ **P**rint
>
> ➠ Page(s): ↵ *(to print all)* or *<range or selected page numbers>* ↵

USAGE

WordPerfect allows you to print documents in a variety of ways, as summarized in Table 4. You can print the document that is currently in RAM (displayed on the screen) or you can print a saved document through the Control Printer screen. In addition, you can print through the List Files screen (F5), or you can print a block of text that you have marked with Block (Alt-F4).

When you select Print, the Print menu appears. (You can also press Ctrl-PrtSc to bring up this menu.) To print the text of the entire document on the screen, select the Full Text option. To print the current page, select the Page option. To print selected pages (in version 5.1), select Multiple Pages and enter the range of pages you want to print. To enter the page range, you type the starting and ending page numbers, separated by a dash, over the *(All)* that appears after the Page(s) prompt. To print from a specific page to the end of the document, enter the starting page number followed by a dash. To print from the beginning of the document up to and including a specific page, enter a dash followed by the ending page number. When entering any of these combinations,

TO PRINT	KEY SEQUENCE
A saved document from the Control Printer screen	Shift-F7 <file name>⏎ ⏎
A range of pages	(for document on screen in version 5.1) Shift-F7 **Multiple Pages** <page numbers to print separated by commas, range of page numbers to print separated by dashes> ⏎ or Shift-F7 <file name> <enter page range> (for document on disk)
A document on the List Files screen	F5 ⏎ [highlight document] **Print**
A group of documents on the List Files screen	F5 ⏎ [highlight each document] * (to mark it) **Print Y**
The entire document on the screen	Shift-F7 **Full Document**
The page on the screen	Shift-F7 **Page**
The text on the screen	Shift-PrtSc

Table 4: WordPerfect's Printing Methods

be sure not to enter any spaces between the numbers and the dash or commas used.

Table 5 shows the various combinations that can be entered at the Page(s) prompt and the results of each.

To print a document that has been saved on disk, select the Document on Disk option from the Print menu and enter the file name of the saved document. Press ↵ to print the whole document, or enter the pages you want to print. In version 5.1 you can choose to print only the document summary by typing S instead of pressing ↵, or you can type S, a comma, and selected page numbers to print a range of pages.

In version 5.0 you cannot print a document on disk that has been Fast Saved unless you move the cursor to the end of the document before you save it, or retrieve it to the screen and print it with the Full Document option. Version 5.1 will automatically run the cursor through a document that has been Fast Saved so that you can print it from disk, but this process takes some time. You can turn off the Fast Save option by using the Setup menu. It is preset to off in version 5.0 and to on in version 5.1.

ENTRY	RESULT
Page(s): 4	Prints only page 4 of the document.
Page(s): 6,12	Prints pages 6 and 12 of the document.
Page(s): 2–6,17	Prints pages 2 through 6 and page 17 of the document.
Page(s): 10–	Prints from page 10 to the end of the document.
Page(s): –5	Prints from the beginning of the document through page 5.
Page(s): x–xii	Prints Roman numeral pages x through xii.
Page(s): iv,2–5,iv–x	Prints the first Roman numeral page iv, Arabic numeral pages 2 through 5, and finally the second Roman numeral pages iv through x.

Table 5: Entering Pages to be Printed

If the document you are printing from disk was formatted for another printer, you will be asked if you want to print the document anyway (version 5.1). If you choose Yes, remember that formatting specific to the original printer may look different on the current printer.

If you did not select a printer when you installed WordPerfect, you will need to do so when you print a document for the first time. WordPerfect saves the printer selection you have made for each document with that document. (In version 5.1 you can specify that retrieved documents be formatted for the printer that is currently selected.)

To select a printer for a document, press Shift-F7 and choose the Select Printer option. When you select a different printer for a document, it is reformatted for that printer. To print a document formatted for a printer other than the one that is attached to your computer, select the printer you want the document to be formatted for. Then print it from disk (using the Document on Disk option on the Print menu or the Print option on the List Files screen) without retrieving it to the screen. This technique lets you get a hard copy of a document formatted for a printer that is not available—for example, if you are working at home with a dot-matrix printer but will print a final draft of your document on a laser printer at work.

If the document you are retrieving has been formatted for a printer that you have not installed (for example, if you are exchanging files with other WordPerfect users), you will see a message indicating that WordPerfect cannot find that particular printer (.PRS) file. It will format the document for your default printer in that case.

Other Print Options

In version 5.0, if your printer supports type-through printing, you can also use the Print menu's Type Through feature to print as though your keyboard were a typewriter, either one character or one line at a time. In version 5.1, the Type Through option is no longer supported.

The View Document option lets you preview your document by pages to see how it will appear when printed.

Headers, footers, notes, graphics, and page numbers will be displayed on the previewed pages.

The Initialize Printer option is used when you download soft fonts. When you choose this option, the fonts you have marked as present when the print job begins (using *) with the Cartridges and Fonts option are downloaded to the printer you have selected.

All of these options are discussed in separate sections. Refer to the See Also list at the end of this entry.

Changing Print Options

Before you print a document, you can temporarily modify the print options that control the printer used, the number of copies printed, the binding width, and the quality of text and graphics. To do this, select one of the options from the lower half of the Print menu:

S - **S**elect Printer

B - **B**inding Offset (**B**inding Width)

N - **N**umber of Copies

U - M**u**ltiple Copies Generated by

G - **G**raphics Quality

T - **T**ext Quality

(Note: The Select Printer and Binding options are discussed in their own separate sections, and the Graphics Quality and Text Quality options are discussed in the **Print Quality** section. The Multiple Copies Generated by option (version 5.1) is discussed under **Print Options**.) Use the Number of Copies option to specify the number of copies of a document to be printed while you work on other documents or begin a new one.

Printing from the List Files Screen

To print a document listed on the List Files screen, move the cursor highlight to the document's name and select the Print option on the List Files menu.

To have WordPerfect consecutively print (batch-print) a group of documents listed on this screen, you must mark each document to be printed by highlighting it and then typing an asterisk (*) to mark it. After you have marked all of the document files you wish to print, select the Print option. When you respond **Y** to the prompt to print the marked files, WordPerfect begins printing the documents in the order in which they were marked. The program places all marked files in its print queue in the order they were marked.

If you need to use printer control at any time, you can press Shift-F7 and go to the Control Printer screen.

To print documents in other subdirectories, highlight the directory name and press ↵ twice; then highlight the document file you want to print and select the Print option. Again, if you want to print a group of files listed in this subdirectory, mark all of the files with an asterisk. To return to the current directory, highlight .. <*Parent*> <*Dir* > and press ↵.

SEE ALSO

Cartridges and Fonts; Font; Printer Control; Print Multiple Pages; Printer, Select; Type Through (version 5.0); View Document.

Printing, Stop

Halts the current printing job.

SEQUENCE OF STEPS

Shift-F7 (Print) *or* ✎ **F**ile pull-down *then* **P**rint

➠ **C**ontrol Printer

➠ **S**top

➠ *[fix printing problem]*

➠ **G**o (start printer)

➠ **F7** (Exit)

USAGE

You may need to stop the printer temporarily to insert a new ribbon or clear a paper jam. To do so, choose the Stop option from the Control Printer screen. This interrupts printing but does not cancel the job. After you have stopped the printer, select the Go option to start it again. If printing does not resume as soon as you select Go, check the message area of the Control Printer screen. You may need to reposition the paper in the printer, for example.

SEE ALSO

Print Job, Cancel.

Printing to Disk

Saves a copy of the document on disk in DOS text or ASCII format.

SEQUENCE OF STEPS

Shift-F7 (Print) *or* 🖱 **F**ile pull-down *then* **P**rint

➠ **S**elect Printer

➠ *[highlight printer name]*

➠ **E**dit

➠ **P**ort

➠ **O**ther

➠ **D**evice or filename: *<name of text file>* ↵

➠ **F7** (Exit) *twice*

➠ **F**ull Document

USAGE ══════════════════

WordPerfect can output a document file to a new disk file rather than to your printer; this is known as printing to a disk. The new disk file created with this operation is essentially a DOS text (ASCII) file that also contains all of the printing control codes required to print it as it was formatted by WordPerfect. To save a file as a DOS text file without the formatting codes, use the Text In/Out key (Ctrl-F5).

When you follow the step sequence shown above, the DOS text file can be printed from the DOS operating system without having a copy of WordPerfect running. This allows you to print WordPerfect documents on a printer attached to another computer that does not even have WordPerfect on it.

As indicated in the step sequence, you need to select the printer name that represents the type of printer that will be used to print the file. Remember that the correct printer definition may differ from the one you use to print documents on the printer (or printers) attached to your computer.

After you specify the printer port, you will need to select the Other option and then type a file name under which the DOS text file version of your document will be stored. If you do not specify a new path name, WordPerfect will save the document in the default directory. When naming the file, you can use the same file name and add the extension .TXT to differentiate it from the original document file.

If you select the DOS Text printer definition, WordPerfect automatically saves the file under the name DOS.TXT.

To obtain a hard copy of the DOS text file, you can use the DOS COPY or PRINT command. (Use COPY if you have temporarily exited from WordPerfect to DOS.)

SEE ALSO ══════════════════

Text In/Out.

Pull-Down Menus

Allows you to select WordPerfect commands and features from menus that appear at the top of the screen instead of using the function keys.

SEQUENCE OF STEPS

Alt-= *or* ↰⊡ *<click right mouse button>*

USAGE

With version 5.1, in addition to the standard function key interface, WordPerfect has a system of pull-down menus that appear when you press the Alt key or the right mouse button.

When you are using pull-down menus, you can use both the keyboard and the mouse in any combination. To select an item from a menu, you can click on it with the left mouse button, or you can type the highlighted mnemonic letter of its name, or you can type the number that corresponds to the position of the item in the menu. You can also press ↵ when an item is highlighted to select it. If selecting an item brings up another pull-down menu, you will see a right-pointing arrowhead at the end of that item. To display the pull-down menu associated with that item, drag the mouse to the item and then release the mouse button or click on the item with the left mouse button. (See **Mouse** for instructions about using the mouse). If an item in a pull-down menu is in brackets, it cannot be selected; for example, you cannot copy or move text until you have marked a block of text.

In pull-down menus, Home ← and Home → move the highlight to the ends of the main menu bar; Home ↑ and Home ↓ (or PgUp and PgDn) move the highlight to the top and bottom of the menus.

Because the items on the pull-down main menu bar are different from the names of the function keys, you will note that in this book an alternate selection is given at the beginning of each step sequence for pull-down menu users. The choices on the main pull-down menu bar are:

File **E**dit **S**earch **L**ayout **M**ark **T**ools **F**ont **G**raphics **H**elp

Once you have chosen from the pull-down menus, you will be in the regular WordPerfect screens. For example, to use the Line Format menu, you select Line from the Layout menu instead of pressing Shift-F8 and typing **1** or **L**. After you select Line, you will see the regular Line Format menu.

To exit from the pull-down menus without selecting anything, press F1 (Cancel), Esc, or the Space bar, or click anywhere with the right mouse button. To exit all the way out of submenus to the editing screen, press F7 (Exit).

Pull-down menus can be used when you are recording a macro; the keystrokes will be recorded just as if you were using the keyboard. However, do not use the mouse to position the cursor when you are recording a macro.

You can use the Setup menu to change how the pull-down menus are displayed on your screen to select whether the Alt key displays the pull-down menus, and to specify that the mouse pointer will automatically go to the menu bar whenever a menu appears (see **Mouse**).

Redline/Strikeout

Allows you to mark text that has been added to the document with redlining and text that has been deleted from it with strikeout.

SEQUENCE OF STEPS

To redline or strike out text as you type it:

Ctrl-F8 (Font) *or* 🖰 **F**ont pull-down

⟶ **A**ppearance

➠ **R**edln; **S**tkout

➠ *<text>* →

To redline or strike out existing text:

Alt-F4 (Block) *or* ␌▭ **E**dit pull-down *then* **B**lock

➠ *[highlight text]*

➠ **Ctrl-F8** (Font) *or* ␌▭ **F**ont pull-down

➠ **A**ppearance

➠ **R**edln; **S**tkout

To select a new redline method for a document:

Shift-F8 (Format) *or* ␌▭ **L**ayout pull-down

➠ **D**ocument

➠ **R**edline Method

➠ **P**rinter Dependent; **L**eft; **A**lternating

➠ **F7** (Exit)

To remove redline markings and strikeout text from the document:

Alt-F5 (Mark Text) *then* **G**enerate *or* ␌▭ **M**ark pull-down

➠ **R**emove Redline Markings and Strikeout Text from Document <Delete redline markings and strikeout text?> **N**o (**Y**es)

➠ **F7** (Exit)

USAGE

Redlining and strikeout are useful features for marking sections of text that have been altered so that others can review the changes quickly without having to check the entire document.

To mark text for redlining (most printers do this by placing a vertical bar in the left margin), select the Redline option. When you have finished typing the text you wish to highlight, press the → key to move beyond the second [redln] format code, or select Font and then Normal to turn off redlining.

To redline text you have already typed, mark the text as a block before you turn on redlining. The way WordPerfect represents redlining on the screen varies according to the type of monitor you are using. It may not be the same way that it will appear in the printed document.

To strike out existing text, mark the text as a block and then select the Strikeout option.

Changing the Redlining Method

You can choose Printer Dependent, Left, or Alternating as the method of redlining. If you choose Printer Dependent, redlining will appear as your printer has defined it; you can test-print a redlined paragraph to see how this appears. The Left option marks redlined text with a horizontal bar in the left margin. The Alternating option marks redlined text on even pages in the left margin and redlined text on odd pages in the right margin.

Deleting Struck-Out Text and Removing Redlining

Before you issue the final version of a document, you will probably want to delete text that has been struck out and remove redlining marks. To do so, press Alt-F5 (Mark Text), choose the Generate option and choose the Remove Redline Markings and Strikeout Text from Document option. When you type Y in response to the prompt, all text between the [STKOUT] and [stkout] codes will be deleted, and the Redline and Strikeout codes will be removed from the document.

SEE ALSO

Document Compare; Print Options.

Retrieve

Retrieves a document on disk or the last text that was cut or copied.

SEQUENCE OF STEPS

To retrieve a document while in the editing screen:

Shift-F10 (Retrieve) *or* ⌨ **File** *then* **Retrieve**

➡ Document to be retrieved: *<document name>* ↵

To retrieve the text most recently moved in the current document:

Shift-F10 (Retrieve) *or* 🖰 **File** t*hen* **Retrieve**

➡ Document to be retrieved: ↵

To retrieve a document from the List Files menu:

F5 (List Files) ↵ *or* 🖰 **File** *then* List Files ↵

➡ *[highlight name of file to be retrieved]*

➡ **R**etrieve

USAGE

To retrieve a saved document, select Retrieve and enter the name of the document; then press ↵. You can also press F5 (List Files) at the Document to be Retrieved: prompt to see the contents of a directory (see **List Files**).

If you do not enter a document name but instead press ↵ at the prompt, the last text you moved or copied from a document you have been working on in the current session will be inserted at the cursor position. You can paste a selection several times by using this feature.

You can also retrieve documents from the List Files menu by selecting its Retrieve option. If you retrieve a document while you are working on another document, you will see the prompt

Retrieve into current document? Yes (**No**)

If you select Yes, the retrieved document will be inserted at the current cursor position, *added to* the current document.

Normally WordPerfect retrieves a document as it was formatted for the printer that was selected when it was saved.

If you try to retrieve a locked document, you will be prompted for a password (see **Locking a File**).

To retrieve a DOS text file, use Text In/Out (Ctrl-F5).

SEE ALSO

Locking a File; Text In/Out.

Reveal Codes

See **Codes**.

Rewrite, Screen

Turns off and on automatic screen rewriting.

SEQUENCE OF STEPS

Ctrl-F3 (Screen)

⇒ **Rewrite**

USAGE

WordPerfect normally rewrites the screen as you enter and edit text so that what you see on the screen resembles what you get in your printed documents. You can temporarily turn off automatic screen formatting to speed up the program's operation if you are working with graphics or complex screen displays.

When you have turned automatic formatting off, you can rewrite the screen by simply pressing Screen (Ctrl-F3) twice.

Save

Saves a document on disk under the name you assign to it.

SEQUENCE OF STEPS

F10 (Save) *or* ⌐ **File** pull-down *then* **S**ave

➠ Document to be saved: *<file name>* ↵

USAGE

To save a file you are working on and then return to it, press Save (F10). WordPerfect will prompt you for a file name if you have not saved the file before. Enter a name of up to eight characters with an optional three-character extension (include a directory and drive designation if you want to save the file somewhere other than the current drive and/or directory); then press ↵.

If you have saved the file previously, WordPerfect will provide its file name when you press Save. To save the file under the same name, press ↵ and respond **Y** to the prompt

Replace *<file name>*? **N**o (**Y**es)

to indicate that you *do* want to replace the original version of the file with the edited version you are now saving. The default setting is No, which allows you to leave the existing file intact and save the new version under another name. If you want to rename the file in order to keep two versions of a document, press ↵ to accept the No setting. WordPerfect will allow you to enter a new file name. Enter the new name (including a drive and directory designation, if you do not want to use the current ones) or edit the existing name; then press ↵.

If you are using long document names (see **Short/Long Document Names**), you will be prompted for a long document name as well as a document type when you save the document. You can enter up to 68 characters, including spaces, for the name and up to 20 characters for the type. If the document has been previously saved, you can save it under the same name by pressing ↵ and choosing **Y** when you are prompted to confirm the replacement. WordPerfect will then show you its version of the DOS file name, abbreviated to eight characters (the type will be indicated by a three-character extension). If you have previously saved the document without using a long document name, that version of its name will be shown as the DOS file name.

You can save a document as DOS text (ASCII format), in generic word processing format (all codes removed except tabs), or in WordPerfect 4.2 format (or 5.0 format if you are using version 5.1) by using the Text In/Out menu (Ctrl-F5, or select Text Out from the File menu).

WordPerfect 5.1 is preset to use the Fast Save option on the Setup menu, which means that it saves a document without formatting it first. This can save you time as you save documents, but it can slow down printing time (see **Fast Save**).

To cancel a save sequence, use the Cancel key (F1).

SEE ALSO

Exit: Saving and Exiting; Text In/Out.

Search

Locates the next occurrence in the document of specified text or formatting codes.

SEQUENCE OF STEPS

To perform a forward search:

F2 (→Search) *or* ⌐⌐ **S**earch pull-down *then* **F**orward

➠ –> Srch: *<search text or function keys>*

➠ **F2** (→Search)

To perform a backward (reverse) search:

Shift-F2 (←Search) *or* **F2** ↑ *or* ⌐⌐ **S**earch pull-down *then* **B**ackward

➠ <– Srch: *<search text or function keys>*

➠ **F2** (→Search)

USAGE

When you select Forward Search, the prompt

–> Srch:

appears at the bottom of your screen. The rightward direction of the arrow indicates that WordPerfect will search for your string of characters from the cursor's present position to the end of the document. After you have entered the search string, press F2 or Esc to carry out the search.

To start a search by using the mouse, select Forward, Backward, Next, or Previous from the Search menu. Enter the search string; then press the right mouse button. The Next and Previous options will search for the next occurrence of the last search string below the cursor (Next) and above it (Previous).

You can include up to 59 characters in the search string. WordPerfect ignores case (capitalization) differences in a search as long as the search string is entered in all lowercase letters. To make a search case-sensitive, enter it using the appropriate capital letters. If you enter characters in uppercase, WordPerfect will search for those characters only as capital letters.

If WordPerfect does not find a match for your search string, it will display the message * *Not Found* *, and the cursor will not move from its original position. In such a case, you can press F2 again and retype or edit the search string.

After WordPerfect finds the first occurrence of your search string, you must repeat the Search command to locate any subsequent occurrences. To reissue the command without changing the search string, press F2 twice. To edit the search string before performing the search again, press F2 once, make your changes, and then press F2 again.

For example, if you enter **file list**, WordPerfect will find all occurrences of *File List*, *file list*, *file List*, and *File list*. If you do not enter a space before *file* and after *list*, WordPerfect will also return any occurrences of the two words together within other words, such as "re*file list*ings." To have WordPerfect search for an entire word by itself, enter a space before and after it.

If you enter **FILE LIST** WordPerfect will search for *FILE LIST* in uppercase letters only.

Canceling a Search Operation

To abort a search operation after entering the search string, press F1 (Cancel). To return to the place in your document where you were before you began a search operation, press Ctrl-Home (Go To) twice.

Using Wild Cards in a Search

You can substitute Ctrl-X for any character when searching for words or phrases in your documents. For example, a search for **no**Ctrl-X returns *now, not, nor, non,* and so forth. It also returns words that contain *now, not, nor, non,* and so forth, such as *nowadays, notable, nonapplicable, enormous, denoted,* and *anonymous.* To enter the wild card (Ctrl-X), press Ctrl-V first. Also note that you cannot use Ctrl-X at the beginning of a search string. Using Ctrl-X as a wild card is useful if you do not remember the exact spelling of the word you wish to find. If you want to limit WordPerfect's search to complete words, you must enter spaces before and after the search string. However, note that this method will not locate words that have a punctuation mark immediately following them.

Extended Searches

When WordPerfect performs a standard search operation, it does not look for matches to your search string in any headers, footers, footnotes, endnotes, graphics box captions, or text boxes that you have added to the document. However, you can perform an extended search operation to include these elements. To do this, press Home before you press F2 to perform a forward search.

With pull-down menus, choose Extended from the Search menu.

Searching in Reverse

You can instruct WordPerfect to search backward through your document to the beginning by pressing Shift-F2 instead of F2 (or by pressing ↑ when the Search prompt is displayed). When you press Shift-F2, WordPerfect responds with this prompt:

<– Srch:

The leftward direction of the arrow shows you that WordPerfect will search from the cursor's present position toward the beginning of the document. After you enter your search string, press Search (F2) to initiate the reverse search, or click the right mouse button. To perform the reverse search operation to locate a previous occurrence, press Shift- F2. To change directions and perform a forward search using the same search string, press the ↓ key when the Search prompt is displayed. You can always change the direction of a search by pressing ↓ or ↑ when you see this prompt.

You can also have WordPerfect perform an extended reverse search by pressing Home before you press Shift-F2 and enter your search string.

Searching for Format Codes

You can also use WordPerfect's Search feature to locate a particular formatting code. (This feature also works while you are using Reveal Codes.) To indicate the code to be searched for, press the appropriate function key or key combination (including, if applicable, the number of the menu option) instead of typing an alphanumeric search string in response to the Search prompt. For instance, to perform a forward search to find the first occurrence of a hard page break, press F2 and then press Ctrl- ↵. In response, the program will display the format code as the search string:

–> Srch: [HPg]

When the code is located, the cursor will be positioned immediately after it.

You can also use this technique to find format codes that require the use of menu options. For example, to search for a [Col On] code, press F2, then press Alt-F7 (Math/Columns) and type **C**.

If you press twice the key that generates a paired code, the Search function will locate the second formatting code of a pair, such as the [undrln] in [UNDRLN][undrln] or the [bold] in [BOLD][bold], so that, for example, you can replace an underlined word or phrase with a boldfaced version of that same word or phrase. If you perform a regular search for one of these paired codes, WordPerfect locates the first (uppercase) code. However, if you press the key for the code twice, the program will locate the second (lowercase) code, which allows you to locate the beginning of a bold word or phrase, mark it as a block, locate its end, and change it to another style or attribute, such as underline or italics.

For example, to search for an [undrln] code, you press F2 and then press Underline (F8) twice. Press ← twice; then press Del to remove the [UNDRLN] code. (If you do not delete the first code, the program will locate only codes with no text between them.)

SEE ALSO

Search and Replace.

Search and Replace

Locates the next occurrence of specified text or formatting codes and replaces them with new text or codes.

SEQUENCE OF STEPS

Alt-F2 (Replace) *or* ⌐ **S**earch pull-down *then* **R**eplace

➧ w/Confirm? **No** (**Yes**)

➧ Srch: *<search text or codes>* **F2** (→Search)

➧ Replace with: *<replacement text or codes>* **F2** (→Search)

USAGE

You can search for words or phrases and replace them with substitute words or phrases that you specify. You can search for up to 59 characters and replace them with as many as 59 characters, including spaces. You can search and replace backward by pressing ↑ before entering the search string.

To perform a search-and-replace operation, select Replace (Alt-F2) or choose Replace from the Search pull-down menu. For an extended replacement that includes headers, footers, endnotes, footnotes, graphics box captions, and text boxes, press Home before you press Alt-F2. WordPerfect then asks you whether you want to confirm each replacement. If you enter **Y**, WordPerfect will ask you to confirm whether you want to make the replacement each time it finds the word or phrase you specified (the *search string*). If you press ↵ to accept the No default selection, WordPerfect will replace each occurrence of the search string without prompting you.

You are then prompted to enter the search string. Press F2 after you enter it. WordPerfect will prompt you to enter the replacement string. You can enter text as well as the following formatting codes if you want them to be inserted in your document:

Appearance; Center; Center Page; Columns On/Off; Font; Hard Space; Hyphen; Hyphenation Cancel; Indent; Justification On/Off; Left-Right Indent; Margin Release; Math On/Off; Math Operators; Merge Code; Size; Soft Hyphen; Tab; Tab Align; Widow/Orphan On/Off

If you do not enter a replacement, WordPerfect will delete all occurrences of the phrase or codes you are searching for.

After you have entered the replacement string, press F2 or click the right mouse button to begin the search-and-replace operation.

Press Cancel (F1) to end a search-and-replace operation.

SEE ALSO

Search.

Short/Long Document Names (Version 5.1)

Allows you to view documents with longer descriptive names.

SEQUENCE OF STEPS

To view long names of documents:

F5 (List Files) *or* ⌐⊟ **File** pull-down *then* List Files

➠ **S**hort/Long Display

➠ **S**hort Display; **L**ong Display

To set long display as the default and specify a default document type:

Shift-F1 (Setup) *or* ⌐ **F**ile pull-down *then* Setup

➠ **E**nvironment

➠ **D**ocument Management/Summary

➠ **L**ong Document Names **Y**es

➠ **F7**

USAGE

In versions of WordPerfect prior to 5.1, you were restricted to the DOS naming conventions (eight characters plus an optional three-character extension) when naming files and directories. In WordPerfect 5.1, you can give a document a more descriptive name when you save or exit; this will be displayed when you have the long display option on in the List Files screen.

To have WordPerfect prompt you to assign long document names, set the Long Document Name option to Yes in the Setup menu by using the step sequence outlined above. From then on, you will be prompted for a long document name as well as a document type (see below) when you save a document or exit. You can use up to 68 characters, including spaces, for the document name and up to 20 characters for the type. After you enter the name and type (or press ↵ to accept what the prompt is showing) WordPerfect will then show you the abbreviated DOS file name for the document; you can edit it if you like. If you have previously assigned the document a name using the normal DOS conventions (eight characters plus an optional three-character extension), this name will be shown at the prompt.

The Document Type is also a new feature in WordPerfect 5.1. It allows you to group related documents together, such as memos, letters, or chapters of different books by assigning them a type. The Document Type appears as a three-character extension of the DOS file name, but it is displayed in its entirety when you are viewing long document names in List Files. You can use the Setup menu to specify a default document type; WordPerfect will then suggest that type as the Document Type when you save the document using long document names.

To retrieve a document by using its long document name, you must use the List Files screen. You cannot enter a long document name when the *Document to be retrieved:* prompt appears (by pressing Shift-F10 in the editing screen or choosing Retrieve from the File menu). To view long document names you have assigned if the List Files screen is not showing the long display, select the Short/Long Display option and choose Long Display.

With Long Display on, WordPerfect must read part of each file in a directory, which can slow down the program, especially in a large directory.

SEE ALSO

Document Summary; List Files.

Sort and Select

Allows you to select and sort lines of text, paragraphs, or secondary merge file records.

SEQUENCE OF STEPS

Ctrl-F9 (Merge/Sort) *or* 🖰 **T**ools

➠ **S**ort

➠ Input file to sort: ↵ *(for screen) or <file name>* ↵

➠ Output file for sort: ↵ *(for screen) or <file name>* ↵

➠ **P**erform Action; **V**iew; **K**eys; **S**elect; **A**ction; **O**rder; **T**ype

---

USAGE	

WordPerfect's Sort feature allows you to perform three kinds of sorting. Each kind calls for its own special formatting:

- For a line sort, data is organized into columns and rows, as in a spreadsheet. Each row forms a record, and each column is separated by a tab.

- For a paragraph sort, the data to be sorted is separated by two (or more) hard returns or a hard page break (Ctrl-↵).

- For a merge sort, the data is in a secondary merge file. Each field is terminated by a Merge R code (^R), and each record in the file is terminated by a Merge E code (^E).

To sort a file by any of these three methods, select Ctrl-F9 (Merge/Sort), or use the Tools pull-down menu, and then select the Sort option. You will then be prompted for the name of the input file to sort. If you press ↵ to accept the default selection (Screen), WordPerfect will sort the file that's in RAM (on your screen). To sort a file that's on disk, enter the complete file name and press ↵.

You are then prompted to indicate where you want the sorted data output. WordPerfect will suggest (Screen) as the output destination. If you wish to save the data in a disk file, enter the file name.

You can also mark a block of text and sort the items in it.

Selecting the Type of Sort

You are then presented with the Sort by Line screen. Sort by Line is the default sort type. To perform a different kind of sort, select the Type option unless your cursor is in a table (in version 5.1). When you do, you are presented with these options:

Sorting Type: **1 M**erge; **2 L**ine; **3 P**aragraph: 0

To select Merge Sort, enter **1** or **M**. To select Paragraph Sort, enter **3** or **P**.

In WordPerfect 5.1 you can sort cells in a table (see **Tables**). If the cursor is in a table when you select Sort, you will see the Table Sort screen. It provides the same features as the other sort screens (defining sort order, defining sort keys, and so forth; see below) but allows you to sort by cell.

Defining the Sort Order

The default sorting order used by WordPerfect is ascending. To change the sort order, select the Order option from the Sort menu. When you do, you are presented with these options:

Sorting Order: **1 A**scending; **2 D**escending: 0

Defining the Sort Keys

To sort data in a file, you must designate the key, or keys, on which to sort it. WordPerfect lets you define up to nine keys for any one sorting operation.

To define the sort key, or keys, to be used, select the Keys option from the Sort menu. You must then define the type of data that will be sorted (alphanumeric or numeric), indicate the field and/or word to be used as the key (fields and words are numbered beginning with 1 from left to right, with words being separated by spaces), and specify the line number to be used (for a paragraph or merge sort).

When you have defined the type of sort, the sort order, and the sort keys to be used, select Perform Action to sort your data. As soon as WordPerfect has sorted your data, the Sort window will disappear, and you will be returned to the full-screen document window.

Selecting the Records to Be Sorted

WordPerfect also allows you to set up conditions that select only certain records. To use the Select feature, you must first define the sort keys that you wish to use. Then choose the Select option from the Sort menu. Enter the condition that must be met, followed by the number of the key to which the condition is applied. When entering the condition, you type the appropriate logical operator after the key number (see Table 6), followed by a value. For example:

    Key1<=650.00*Key1>=2500.00

specifies those records in which Key1 (an amount-due field) is between $650.00 and $2500.00. The asterisk (*) indicates the logical AND operator.

After you enter your selection condition, press Exit (F7) to return to the Sort menu. Select Perform Action to have WordPerfect select and sort your records.

WordPerfect also lets you select records without sorting them. To do this, you still must define the necessary keys and enter the selection condition as previously described. However, before you select Perform Action, select the Action option. When you do this, WordPerfect presents these options:

    Action: **1 S**elect and Sort; **2** Select **O**nly: 0

Select the Select Only option. When you choose the Perform Action option, WordPerfect will eliminate all records that do not meet the selection condition, although their arrangement will be unchanged from the order in which they were originally entered.

SYMBOL	FUNCTION	EXAMPLE
=	Equal to	key1=IL
<>	Not equal to	key1<>CA
>	Greater than	key1>M
<	Less than	key2<50.00
>=	Greater than or equal to	key1>=74500
<=	Less than or equal to	key2<=H
*	Logical AND	key1=IL * key2<60600
+	Logical OR	key1=IL + key3>1000.00
g	Global selection	key g=Mary

Table 6: Symbols and Logical Operators Used in Sorting Records

Changing the Sorting Sequence (Version 5.0)

To change the sorting sequence, press Ctrl-F9 and select Sort Order. You are then presented with these options:

Sort Order: **1 U**S/European; **2 S**candinavian: 0

To select the Scandinavian sorting sequence, which contains more than 26 letters, press **2** or **S**. To return to the US/European sorting sequence (the normal dictionary sort order for languages using the Roman alphabet without any foreign-language characters), press **1** or **U**.

SEE ALSO

Merge Operations.

Speller

Allows you to check the spelling of a word, a block of text, or an entire document.

SEQUENCE OF STEPS

Ctrl-F2 (Spell) *or* ⌐ **T**ools pull-down *then* **S**pell

➠ **W**ord; **P**age; **D**ocument; **N**ew Sup. Dictionary; **L**ook Up; **C**ount

USAGE

WordPerfect's Speller key (Ctrl-F2, or **S**pell on the **T**ools menu) allows you to check your documents for typographical errors and misspellings. In version 5.1, the Speller also checks for certain types of incorrect capitalization. Its main dictionary contains over 100,000 words, and it automatically creates a supplemental dictionary that contains all the words you add to the dictionary as you write.

If you are using the Speller on a floppy disk system, you must first insert the Speller disk into drive B. *Note:* In version 5.1 you must have high-density floppy drives (720K or higher).

You can choose whether to check the word the cursor is on, the current page, or the entire document. You can also check the spelling in text you have marked with Block (Alt-F4).

Checking a Word

To check the spelling of the word the cursor is on, select Spell (press Ctrl-F2 or use the Tools pull-down menu) and select Word. If the cursor moves to the next word, the current word is spelled correctly. If the spelling is incorrect, WordPerfect will present a list of any possible alternatives. Press the letter corresponding to the word you wish to use or, if the correct alternative is not displayed, press → to begin editing the word manually.

Checking a Page

To check for misspellings and typographical errors only on the page in which the cursor appears, use the Page option. You may want to do this if you have checked the entire document and then made corrections or additions to a certain page.

Checking a Document

The Document option allows you to check your entire document, including headers, footers, footnotes, and endnotes.

Changing Dictionaries

By selecting the New Sup. Dictionary option, you can specify that WordPerfect check a custom dictionary that you have created. To create a new supplemental dictionary, simply create a new document containing the words you want to include, each separated by a hard return. *Make sure that the words are spelled correctly.* When you save the document, give it a name, such as LEGAL.SUP, that helps you remember that it is a supplemental dictionary. Then enter that name when you are prompted for the name of a supplemental dictionary after selecting this option.

To create custom main dictionaries, use the Speller Utility, a separate program contained on the Speller/Thesaurus disk.

You can specify the directory in which your dictionaries are stored by using the Location of Files option on the Setup menu.

Looking Up an Alternative Spelling

To look up alternative spellings of a word, select the Look Up option and type a word or word pattern at the prompt. WordPerfect then presents all the close combinations of that pattern it can find in its dictionaries.

When you look up a word, you can use the question mark (?) and asterisk (*) wild-card characters in place of letters you are unsure of. The question mark stands for any one letter, and the asterisk represents a sequence of letters. For example, type **rec??ve** to see whether *receive* is spelled as *receive* or *recieve*.

Getting a Word Count

To obtain a quick count of the number of words in a document, use the Count option of the Speller menu. This option works without spell-checking the document. A count is also given after each spell check.

Using the Speller

When you use the Speller, WordPerfect checks your document for words it does not recognize. When it encounters one of these, it presents the message *Not Found* and displays a list of possible spellings (if it finds any near matches). You can simply press the letter corresponding to the correct word; WordPerfect inserts it into the document for you.

The Speller ignores numbers, but it will query alphanumeric words, such as *F3*.

WordPerfect's Speller also locates words that occur twice in a row and presents the following menu:

Double word: **1 2 S**kip; **3** Delete 2nd; **4** Edit; **5** Disable
   Double Word Checking

You can choose Delete 2nd to delete the second occurrence, or you can leave the words in place (choose Skip). Disable Double Word Checking allows you to turn this feature off so that the program does not query you at double words.

Once you've selected the Page or Document option of the Speller, the standard menu you see when a word is being queried contains five options:

1 Skip Once; **2** Skip; **3** Add Word; **4** Edit; **5** Look Up; **6**
   Ignore Numbers

Skipping a Word

If you instruct the Speller to skip a word once, it will query you the next time it locates the pattern in your document. Use Skip if you want to keep a certain spelling in this document but do not want to add it to the dictionary. You will not be queried on that spelling again during the current session with the Speller.

Adding a Word

To add a word that is being queried—such as a proper name or a specialized term—to the dictionary as you are correcting a document, select Add Word. WordPerfect will then add it to the supplemental dictionary that is automatically created as you use the Speller.

You can also add words to the supplemental dictionary directly by retrieving the file WP{WP}EN.SUP and typing each word that you wish to add, separated by a hard return. Be sure to save the file under the same name after you have added words to it. (While you have the file on the screen, you can also correct any misspelled words that may have been inadvertently added to the supplemental dictionary.)

Editing a Word

If you choose Edit, you may edit the word that is presented or simply use the → or ← key to move from that word to the part of the sentence or paragraph that you wish to edit. While you are working with the Speller, only the → and ← keys, along with Backspace and Del, are available as cursor movement keys. You cannot use most of the other cursor movement techniques, such as Go To (Ctrl-Home), or End. You can change from Insert to Typeover mode, however.

After you have edited a word in your document, press Exit (F7) to return to the Speller.

Looking Up a Word

By selecting this option while you are checking a document, you can enter a word that you wish WordPerfect to look up. Type a word or word pattern at the prompt. WordPerfect then presents all of the close matches to the word that it can find in its dictionaries.

Ignoring Numbers

WordPerfect's Speller will stop and query alphanumeric combinations such as F1. If you want it to ignore words that contain numbers, select Ignore Numbers the first time it queries such a combination. (Use the Add option to add alphanumeric words you use frequently to the dictionary.)

Checking Capitalization (Version 5.1)

Version 5.1's Speller will also query you if it comes across a word whose first two letters are capitalized, such as "YOu", or a word whose first letter is lowercase and second letter is capitalized, such as "yOu". Choose Replace to have the second capitalized letter changed to lowercase, or choose Disable to disable case checking.

Exiting from the Speller

To exit from the Speller, press Cancel (F1). The program will present a count of the text it has checked up to that point. Save your document if you want the changes introduced with the Speller to be incorporated into the saved version.

SEE ALSO

Hyphenation; Thesaurus.

Spreadsheet (Version 5.1)

Allows you to import data from spreadsheet files.

SEQUENCE OF STEPS

To import data from a spreadsheet (one time only):

Ctrl-F5 (Text In/Out) *or* ⌨ File pull-down *then* Text In

➡ **Spreadsheet**

➡ **Import**

➡ **Filename** *<enter name and press ↵ or press F5 to see list>*

➡ **R**ange *<enter range of cells to import>*

➡ **T**ype

➡ **T**able; **T**ext

➡ **P**erform Import

To link a spreadsheet to the current document:

Ctrl-F5 (Text In/Out) *or* ▭ **F**ile *then* Text **I**n

➡ **S**preadsheet

➡ **C**reate Link

➡ **F**ilename *<enter filename and press ↵ or press F5 to see list>*

➡ **R**ange

➡ **T**ype

➡ **T**able *or* **T**ext

➡ **P**erform Link

To specify link options after creating a link:

Ctrl-F5 (Text In/Out) *or* ▭ **F**ile pull-down *then* Text **I**n

➡ **S**preadsheet

➡ **L**ink Options

➡ **U**pdate on **R**etrieve **N**o *then* **F7** (Exit); **S**how Link Codes **Y**es *then* **F7** (Exit); **U**pdate All Links

---

USAGE

WordPerfect 5.1 allows you to import spreadsheet data from Lotus 1-2-3 (pre-3.0 versions) and PlanPerfect, WordPerfect Corporation's spreadsheet program. You can import an entire spreadsheet or a range of cells. In addition, you can create a link to a spreadsheet file that automatically updates the spreadsheet in your document as you update it in the spreadsheet program.

When you are importing spreadsheets, you can press F5 and ↵ to see the List Files screen for the current directory, or you can edit the path name to view another directory where you store spreadsheet files. You can also use wild card characters to specify that you view only spreadsheet files. For example, editing the path name from C:\WP51*.* to C:\WP51*.WK1 will display only the Lotus 1-2-3 files that are in the WP51 directory in the List Files screen. Likewise, you can press F5 when you are specifying a range of cells to import to see any ranges you have defined in your spreadsheet. To enter an unnamed range, enter the cell address of the upper left corner of the block of cells you want to import, type a colon (:), and enter the cell address of the lower right corner of the block of cells—for example, A1:D10.

You can choose whether you want the data imported as a table or as text. No matter which you choose, you will be able to edit the data once it is in WordPerfect. If you import it as a table, it can be edited like a WordPerfect table (see **Tables**). If you import it as text, the spreadsheet cells are separated by tabs and rows are separated by hard returns.

If the spreadsheet extends beyond the right margin of the page size you are using, you will get a warning message. If you have imported the spreadsheet as a table, the cells that will not fit on the page are not displayed; if you have imported it as text, the cells are wrapped to the next line at the right margin. If this happens, you can print the page in Landscape mode (lengthwise on the page), change the right and left margin settings, or edit the data to break it into smaller tables.

You can also import a spreadsheet into a graphics box (see Graphics) as long as it will fit on one page.

Linking a Spreadsheet

If you link a spreadsheet, changes that are made to it while it is in the spreadsheet program will be reflected in the linked data in your document. WordPerfect will automatically retrieve the linked data when you select Perform Link.

Before you link a spreadsheet to a document, you can specify certain link options, as outlined in the step sequence above. The program is preset not to update a linked spread-sheet each time you retrieve the document; to have Word-Perfect automatically update the linked spreadsheet when you retrieve the document, set this option to Yes. To update links while you are working in WordPerfect, select the Up-date All Links option. When you do so, any changes that were made and saved in the linked spreadsheet after you retrieved the document will be updated.

WordPerfect normally displays nonprinting Link: and Link End: codes at the points where a link begins and ends. You can set the Show Link Codes option to No to suppress this display.

Although linked data can be edited in WordPerfect, you should not edit it until you are sure it is in final form and that the spreadsheet will not need to be updated again. When you update a linked spreadsheet, you will lose any editing changes that you made to it previously. The linked spreadsheet data will be in the base font that is in effect in the document; you may, for example, want to change text attributes and sizes or use a different font for the data. Wait until you are sure that no further changes will be made to the spreadsheet.

SEE ALSO

Tables.

Styles

You can store sets of formatting commands that can be ap-plied to various parts of your document.

SEQUENCE OF STEPS

To create or edit a style:

Alt-F8 (Style) *or* ⌐ Layout pull-down *then* **S**tyle

➡ **C**reate *or* **E**dit

➠ **N**ame; **T**ype; **D**escription; **C**odes; **E**nter

➠ **F7** (Exit)

To apply a style in the document:

[Position cursor where you want to apply style]

➠ **Alt-F8** (Style)

➠ *[Highlight style name]*

➠ **O**n

➠ *<text>*

➠ **O**ff *or* ↵ (*if you defined* ↵ *as Off*)

USAGE

You can set up styles for each element in your document and use the style instead of formatting text as you type. For example, you can use one style for quotations, and you can define other styles for each level of heading you are using in your documents. For instance, if you want all level-1 headings to be boldfaced and centered, you can define that style. Then, when you are typing a level-1 heading in your text, you can simply turn on the style instead of pressing F6 for bold and Shift-F6 for center. If you work with complex design elements, such as multicolumn formats and a variety of type styles, this feature can save you many keystrokes throughout a document.

WordPerfect 5.1 comes with several predefined styles for a bibliography, two types of documents, a legal pleading, and right-justified paragraph numbers. You can use these styles, edit them for your own purposes, or create new styles.

Style Types

You can use two different types of styles in WordPerfect 5.0: *paired* and *open*. In version 5.1, you can also use an outline style that is used with paragraph and outline numbers; you can define a style for each level of numbering (see **Using Outline Styles** below). In a paired style, the codes are turned on and then turned off at the end of the text element, such as turning off bold at the end of the heading or returning to normal size after a quotation in smaller type. Open styles are not turned off, so they are appropriate for setting the style of an entire document, such as margins, justification, line spacing, and so forth.

Creating a Style

To create a style:

1. Select the Style menu.

2. Select Create; then select Name.

3. Enter a descriptive name for the style, such as **1 head** (for level-1 headings). You can use up to 11 characters.

4. To select whether the style is to be paired or open, select Type; then select Open or Paired.

5. To enter a description of the style you are creating, select Description; then enter a short description (up to 54 characters) of the style.

6. You can use both text and codes in a style. To indicate to WordPerfect which codes you want generated when you use this style, select Codes and press the appropriate keys to generate the codes. For example, if you want level-1 heads to be centered and boldfaced, press Center (Shift-F6) and Bold (F6). If you are defining a paired style, type the codes that are to be used when the style is turned on *before* the [Comment] on the screen. Move the cursor past the comment and then type the codes that you want WordPerfect to generate when the style is turned off *after* the [Comment]. For example, to insert boldfacing codes, press Bold (F6) to generate the [BOLD] code; then press → to move past the [Comment]. Press F6 again to generate the [bold] code. If the style is being used to mark

text—as for an index or table of contents heading, for example—press Block (Alt-F4) before the [Comment], move the cursor past the [Comment], and then press the appropriate keys to generate the correct Mark Text code. For example, to mark a heading for a level-1 table of contents entry, you would press Alt-F5, choose ToC, and enter **1** for level 1.

In WordPerfect 5.1, you can insert graphics in a style. Press Alt-F9 (Graphics) or choose Graphics from the pull-down menu; then select the type of graphics box you want to use—Figure, Table, User-Defined, Line, or Equation (see **Graphics**). Press Exit (F7) when you have defined the style.

7. If you are creating a paired style, you can assign it to the ⏎ key by choosing Enter and selecting an option for the way the ⏎ key is to function. You can choose to have the ⏎ key turn off the style, or you can have it turn the style on and then turn it off again. Press Exit (F7) to return to the Style menu.

For a quick way to create a style in an existing document, mark as a block (Alt-F4) the codes that generate the style you want to define; then select Style and the Create option. When you select Codes, you will see that WordPerfect has created a paired style from the codes you have highlighted. You can then edit these codes. Be sure to name your new style so that you can remember what it does.

Using Outline Styles (Version 5.1)

In version 5.1, a new style type, Outline, has been added. Outline styles are used with outlining and paragraph numbering, which can have up to eight levels. By using the

Outline styles feature, you can specify a style for each of these numbering levels.

You can set up an outline style by using either the Date/Outline menu or the Styles menu. After you select Outline as the style type on the Styles:Edit menu, you will be asked to give the style a name and indicate a level (1 through 8). You will then be taken to the Outline Styles:Edit menu, which is the same menu that appears when you use the Date/Outline menu to define an outline style. You can then assign specific styles to each of the eight numbering levels, choosing whether they are to be paired or open, assigning the action of the Enter key, and specifying text and codes, just as you do for a "regular" style, as discussed below. After you have set up an outline style, WordPerfect will follow it when you use paragraph and outline numbering. You can change to different levels of outline styles by pressing Shift-Tab and Tab, just as you do with paragraph numbering (see **Outlining** and **Paragraph Numbering**).

Editing a Style

After you have created a style, you can use the Style menu's Edit option to edit it:

1. Select Style and highlight the style you want to change.

2. Choose Edit and edit the style.

3. Press Exit (F7) when you have finished editing the style.

WordPerfect automatically changes the codes in your document to conform to the edited style after you have changed it.

To delete a style, highlight it and select Delete; then type **Y** to confirm the deletion.

Applying a Style

To use an open style you have created, press Style (Alt-F8), use the arrow keys to move the cursor to the style, and select On. Then type the text that you want to appear in that style. When you apply an open style, it will affect the entire document from the cursor's position forward.

If you are applying a paired style, press Style (Alt-F8), use the arrow keys to move the cursor to the style, then select On. When you reach the end of the text you want to have in that style, press Alt-F8 and select Off. Or, if you have assigned the Off or Off/On option to the ↵ key, press ↵ to turn off the style.

If you are using a paired style, you can also block the text you want to apply the style to and then apply the style as described above. WordPerfect automatically inserts the Style On and Style Off codes around the blocked text.

Saving and Retrieving Styles

The styles you define for a document are saved with the document. You can save the styles as a separate document, however, so that you can apply them to several different documents without having to define styles in each one. To do this, choose Save from the Style menu and enter a name for the list of styles displayed on the screen. Then, to retrieve those styles into another document, choose Retrieve from the Style menu and enter the name of the style list.

If you retrieve a style list into a document that already has a list of styles, you will be prompted as to whether you want to replace the document's existing styles with the new ones that you are retrieving. Type **N** to retrieve only the styles that have different names from the ones in the current document, or type **Y** to replace the list on the screen with the list you are retrieving.

Suppress Page Format

Allows you to suppress the printing of page numbers or headers and footers for the current page.

SEQUENCE OF STEPS

Shift-F8 (Format) *or* ⌨ **L**ayout pull-down

➡ **P**age

➡ **S**uppress (this page only)

➡ Suppress **A**ll Page Numbers, Headers, and Footers

Suppress Headers and Footers

Print Page Numbers at **B**ottom Center

Suppress **P**age Numbering

Suppress **H**eader A

Suppress H**e**ader B

Suppress **F**ooter A

Suppress F**o**oter B

➡ **F7** (Exit)

USAGE

To suppress headers, footers, and/or page numbers on a single page, position the cursor at the top of the page (just under the dashed line that marks the page break on your screen). Then press Shift-F8 or select the Layout pull-down menu and choose the Page option followed by Suppress for Current Page Only. Then select the features (or the combination of features) you want to suppress.

To restore a suppressed format, locate the page with the [Suppress] code and delete that code.

SEE ALSO

Headers and Footers; Page Numbering.

Switch Document

Switches between the Doc 1 and Doc 2 editing screens.

SEQUENCE OF STEPS

Shift-F3 (Switch) *or* ⌐ **E**dit pull-down *then* **S**witch Document

USAGE

If the "Block on" message is displayed (indicating that text has not been marked as a block), pressing Switch (Shift-F3) switches you to a second document window. Pressing it a second time returns you to the original document window. You can work with another document or another version of the same document in each window.

NOTE

If you have marked text as a block, pressing Switch displays the Conversion menu so that you can switch to uppercase or lowercase.

SEE ALSO

Case Conversion; Windows.

Tab Align

Aligns text on or around the next tab stop using the decimal/align character in effect.

SEQUENCE OF STEPS

Ctrl-F6 (Tab Align) *or* ⌐ **L**ayout pull-down *then* **A**lign *then* **T**ab Align

USAGE

Tab Align aligns text on or around a tab setting using the alignment character that is in effect. WordPerfect uses the period as the alignment character unless you specify another character or symbol. You can use the Tab Align command with any tab stop that is in effect.

Characters that you type after pressing Tab Align are inserted to the left of the cursor, and the cursor remains stationary at the tab stop until you type the alignment character.

To change the alignment character from the period to another character—for example, the colon (:)—follow these steps:

1. Press Format (Shift-F8) and choose the Other option.

2. Choose Decimal/Align Char and enter the character you want to use as the alignment character—in this case, the colon (:). Press ↵, then press Exit (F7) to return to your document.

3. To then align your text on the colon, press the Tab key until you are only one tab stop away from where you want the text aligned.

4. Press Ctrl-F6. The cursor will advance to the next tab stop, and you will see this message at the bottom of the screen: *Align Char = :*

As you type your text, it will be entered from right to left, just as it is when you use a right-justified or decimal tab. As soon as you type the alignment character—in this case, the colon— the *Align Char = :* message disappears, and any text you then type is entered from left to right as though you were using a left-justified tab. Pressing Tab again or pressing ↵ leaves text aligned and simply moves the cursor.

To return text that was aligned with the Tab Align command to the previous tab stop, access the Reveal Codes screen (Alt-F3) and delete the [Align] or [C/A/Flrt] formatting codes that surround the aligned text. If you press Backspace when the cursor is located on one of these codes, you will see a message asking you to confirm the deletion. If you wish to retain the current alignment, press ↵. If you do not, type **Y**.

SEE ALSO

Decimal/Align Character.

Tables

Wordperfect 5.1 allows you to create columns and rows of text easily.

SEQUENCE OF STEPS

To create a table:

   Alt-F7 (Columns/Tables) *or* ▭ **L**ayout pull-down

   ➡ **T**ables

   ➡ **C**reate *<enter number of columns>* ↵ *<enter number of rows>* ↵

To edit a table:

   Alt-F7 (Columns/Tables) *or* **L**ayout pull-down

   ➡ **T**ables

➠ **E**dit

➠ **S**ize; **F**ormat; **L**ines; **H**eader; **M**ath; **O**ptions;
Join; **Sp**lit

➠ **F7** (Exit)

To format individual cells or groups of cells when the Table Edit menu is displayed:

Format

➠ **C C**ell (**T**ype; **A**ttributes; **J**ustify; **V**ertical Alignment;
Lock); **C**olumn (**W**idth; **A**ttributes; **J**ustify; **# D**igits);
Row Height (**Single Line: F**ixed; Auto; **Multi-Line:**
Fi**x**ed; **A**uto)

USAGE

WordPerfect 5.1's Tables feature allows you to manipulate data in columns and rows easily. The automatic Math feature in the tables allows you to apply formulas to the columns and rows, a useful feature for creating forms such as invoices and order sheets. The tables feature is also valuable in documents that use reference aids, since you can also use most of WordPerfect's Mark Text features, such as footnotes and endnotes, index, and tables of contents.

A table can have as many as 32 columns and 765 rows. Once you have set up your basic table structure, you can begin entering data in the cells. Press F7 to remove the Table Edit menu and begin typing in cells. (To redisplay the menu, press Alt-F7, or choose Tables and Edit from the Layout pull-down menu.) While the cursor is in the table, the status line reflects the cell position. To move to the next cell in the same row, press Tab; to insert a tab indent in a cell, press Home then Tab. (For other cursor-movement techniques in tables, see your reference manual.) You can also point and click with the mouse to move directly to a cell, or scroll a table to see a cell that is not displayed on the screen. As you enter characters within a cell, the cell will expand to hold what you are typing. All the cells across the row will expand by the same amount. To format individual cells or groups of cells, use the Format Cell option (see below).

WordPerfect considers a table to be a table graphics box and numbers it accordingly with its automatic list-numbering feature (see **Lists**). If you are using the Cross-Reference feature to create an automatic reference, remember that your table is actually a graphics box and select Graphics Box Number as the reference type (see **Cross-Reference**).

To create a table from text that you have already typed, mark it as a block, press Alt-F7 and choose Tables (or choose Tables from the Layout menu); then select Create. Items that were separated by tabs will be in columns; lines that were separated by hard returns will be in rows.

To delete a table, mark it as a block and press Del or Backspace; then type **Y** in response to the *Delete Block?* prompt. To delete a table's structure but leave its text within the document, locate and delete the [Table Def] code that corresponds to the table.

Note that you can import a spreadsheet or a range of data into a table without setting up a table structure first (see **Spreadsheet**).

Editing Tables

When you choose to edit a table, the program searches backward from the cursor to the nearest table and displays the table editing screen. You can also simply move the cursor to a location within the table you want to edit; then press Alt-F7 to display the table editing screen quickly. In the table editing screen, you will see the following menu:

Ctrl-Arrows Column Widths; **Ins** Insert; **Del** Delete;
    Move Move/Copy; **1 S**ize; **2 F**ormat; **3 L**ines;
    4 Header; **5 M**ath; **6 O**ptions; **7 J**oin; **8 Sp**lit

You can change column widths by pressing Ctrl and →
or ← while the cursor is within the column you want to
widen or shorten. To add a row or column, press Ins and
select Rows or Columns; this inserts a copy of the current
row or column before the column or above the row where
the cursor is. Pressing Del and choosing Rows or Columns deletes the row or column where the cursor is, including any text that is in the cells. You can restore it with

the F1 (Cancel) key. You can also use the Size option to change the number of rows and columns in the table. In addition, if you have an enhanced keyboard, you can add or delete rows in normal editing mode by pressing Ctrl-Del or Ctrl-Ins.

To move or copy a column or row, display the Table Edit, then press Ctrl-F4 (Move) when the cursor is in the column or row you want to work with or after you have blocked the cells you want to cut or copy. This feature works like the Move feature in the normal editing screen: you can choose to move or copy a row, column, or block; press ↵ to retrieve it at its new location.

The Size option allows you to add and delete rows and columns from the end of a table. After you select Size, you can choose either Rows or Columns. WordPerfect will display the number of rows (or columns) that are currently in the table. Add the number of rows (or columns) you want to add to the table to this number, then enter the total number. For example, if you want to add two rows to a five-row table, enter **7**. To delete rows and columns, subtract the number you want to delete from the number that WordPerfect displays. Rows and columns at the end (bottom and right) of the table will be deleted, along with any text that is in them. Columns and rows that you delete with this option cannot be restored with the F1 (Cancel) key.

Use the Lines option to determine the types of lines (also called rules or borders) that you want to have printed around the table. WordPerfect treats these lines as graphics, so if your printer cannot print graphics, your printed tables will not have lines. You will see the following menu:

Lines: 1 Left; **2** Right; **3** Top; **4** Bottom; **5** Inside;
6 Outside; **7** All; **8** Shade

After you select the lines you want to change, you can choose from the following options:

1 None; **2** Single; **3** Double; **4** Dashed; **5** Dotted;
6 Thick; **7** Extra Thick

The Shade option allows you to turn shading on and off in the cell where the cursor is or in the group of cells you have highlighted. To set the percentage of shading, use Options (see below).

If a table is too long to fit on one page, WordPerfect will carry it to the next page, breaking it at a row. You can use the Header feature to repeat a row of information at the top of each page. You will not see this header displayed on subsequent pages unless you use the View Document option. However, the status line will show an asterisk next to the cell location on the status line when the cursor is in a header row.

To protect an area of a table from being broken between pages, mark as a block the rows that should not be broken and press Shift-F8 (Format) or choose Protect Block from the Edit menu, which turns on block protection.

WordPerfect assumes that the Math feature is on in tables. If you select Math, you can enter formulas and make calculations (see Using Math in Tables below).

To specify how your table is to be displayed, select Options. You will then see a menu that lets you specify the exact spacing between text and lines and specify the percentage of gray shading to use when shading is turned on for a cell; the default is 10%. It also lets you choose whether negative numbers are to be displayed with a leading minus sign or in parentheses, as some financial applications use.

In addition, you can choose how the table is positioned on the page by using the Position option. Normally WordPerfect aligns the table with the left margin, but you can choose Right (to align it with the right margin), Center (to center it between the margins), Full (to adjust its width to fill the space between the margins), or Set Position (to enter an offset from the left margin). When WordPerfect first creates a table, all the columns are a fixed size, so that the table appears to occupy all the space between the margins, but as you adjust the size of columns by sizing them or entering text into them, you will see the table change in size. If you are using a Left position, the table will shrink toward the left margin as you decrease the size of a column in it.

The Join and Split options let you join several cells that you have highlighted or split a cell into several rows or columns. If you join multiple cells, text that was in them will be separated with tabs to indicate where the column breaks were and hard returns where the rows were. If you split a cell, you will be prompted to choose whether you want to split it into rows or columns, and how many you want to have. Any text that is in a split cell will remain in the first cell after the split.

Formatting Columns and Cells

You can mark a group of cells as a block and apply format changes to them, or you can format an individual cell or column. In addition, you can set row height for a row of cells. When you use the Format option on the table editing screen, you will see the following menu:

1 Cell; **2 C**olumn; **3 R**ow Height

Formatting Cells

If you choose Cell, you can select from the following choices:

Cell: **1 T**ype; **2 A**ttributes; **3 J**ustify; **4 V**ertical Alignment; **5 L**ock

The first option, Type, allows you to specify whether a cell contains text or is numeric (the default). Numeric cells can be used in calculations, but if you have cells that contain information that will never be calculated, such as phone numbers, you can specify those cells as text.

Attributes allows you to set size and appearance attributes for the cell or group of cells. However, you can bold or underline information in a cell without using this option; move the cursor to the cell and press F6 (Bold) or F8 (Underline).

Justify allows you to specify left, center, right, full, or decimal alignment for the text in the cell(s). Select Reset to return the alignment in the cell to whatever alignment is being used in the column.

Vertical Alignment lets you specify Top, Bottom, or Center (the default) as the method for displaying text vertically in the cell. Any changes you make will not be apparent on the screen, but you will be able to see them in View Document or when you print the document.

Lock lets you protect a cell's contents from being changed. Nothing can be entered into a locked cell once it has been locked. When the cursor is in a locked cell, its cell address is shown in brackets on the status line.

Formatting Columns

If Column is selected, the menu appears as:

1 Width; **2 A**ttributes; **3 J**ustify; **4 # D**igits

The first option, Width, lets you specify a column width. Normally WordPerfect calculates the distance between the right and left margins and then divides that width by the number of columns you want in the table. This option overrides that setting. You can also change column widths without using the Table Edit menu (but when it is displayed) by simply pressing Ctrl-→ or Ctrl-← when the cursor is within the column whose width you want to change.

Attributes lets you set size and appearance attributes for the column; Normal turns off any column attributes that you have set.

Justify allows you to specify justification for the column. The choices are the same as for cells (see above).

The last option, # Digits, lets you specify the number of decimal places that will be treated as significant in calculations. It does not limit the number of digits that can be entered in the cells in the column.

Changing Row Height

If you choose Row Height, you will see the following menu:

Row Height—Single Line: 1 Fixed; **2 A**uto;
   Multi-Line: 3 Fixed; **4 A**uto

Normally WordPerfect automatically calculates the height of a row of cells so that all the text that is in the cells will display and print properly. However, you can override this setting for either a single row of cells or several rows that you

have first marked as a block. WordPerfect will convert whatever you enter to inches (the default unit of measurement)
unless you have changed the default unit of measurement
or unless you enter the number followed by an abbreviation indicating a different unit of measurement. If the text
in a row will not fit in the fixed height you enter, it will not
be displayed or printed, but it will still be there if you later
change back to automatic row height or enter a row height
that will accommodate the text. Use the Single Line settings for rows in which you want text to have only one
line per cell; use Multi-Line for rows in which cells can
contain more than one line of text.

Using Math in Tables

If you have used WordPerfect's Math feature before, you will
already be familiar with the Math feature that is found in
Tables, although you may find it somewhat easier to use since
all you have to do is specify formulas that are to operate on
groups of cells. In addition to using the basic Math functions
(add, subtract, multiply, and divide), once you have set up a
formula in a cell, you can copy it into other cells.

Formulas that you enter may reference any cell that is in
the table, such as A4+B5*.065 (to calculate 6.5% sales tax on
data in cells A4 and B5, for example), or may simply be a calculation that does not use any cell, such as 4*23.5. To enter a
formula such as B1+B2 (which will add whatever you enter
in cell B1 to whatever you enter in cell B2), move the cursor
to the cell that you want to hold the formula, press Alt-F7 to
bring up the table editing screen, choose Math, and then
choose Formulas. You will see an *Enter/Formula:* prompt.
Enter the formula, using the operators +, −, /, *, and = (you
cannot use %; enter percentages as a decimal number).
When you press ↵, the formula will be entered into the cell.
The formula will be shown at the bottom-left corner of the
screen when the cursor is in the cell.

It is possible to enter data into cells that contain formulas.
However, WordPerfect will not calculate the results of formulas in a table until you select Calculate from the Math
menu, so the table on the screen may display erroneous

results until you calculate it. Also, to be used correctly in calculations, text that is in cells must be numeric.

Once you have set up a formula, you can copy it into other cells by using Copy Formula. You will then need to enter the cell address where you want to copy the formula. Select Cell and enter a cell address, or, if you want to copy the formula into several contiguous cells, select Down or Right and enter the number of times you want the formula copied. The formula will be copied relative to its new address; for example, if the original formula is A1+A2 and you copy it down two rows, the new formulas will be A2+A3 and A3+A4.

If you add, move, or delete columns that are used in calculations, you will need to revise the formulas that involve them.

The special operators +, =, and * can be used to create subtotals (+), totals (=), and grand totals (*). They work just as they do with the Math feature (see **Math**). However, in tables you must enter these operators by selecting them from the menu after you select Math.

SEE ALSO

Graphics; Math; Spreadsheet.

Tables of Authorities

Allows you to generate in a legal document a list of citations that is automatically maintained by WordPerfect.

SEQUENCE OF STEPS

To mark the full form for the table:

Alt-F4 (Block) *or* ⌐ **E**dit pull-down *then* **B**lock

➡ *[highlight text to be cited]*

➡ **Alt-F5** (Mark Text) *then* To **A** *or* ⌐ **M**ark
pull-down *then* Table of **A**uthorities *then* Mark **F**ull

➠ ToA Section Number (Press Enter for Short Form only): *<section number between 1 and 16>* ↵

➠ *[enter full form]* **F7**

➠ Short Form: *<short form name>* ↵

To define the style of the table of authorities:

Alt-F5 (Mark Text) *or* ⌨ **M**ark pull-down

➠ **D**efine

➠ Define Table of **A**uthorities

➠ *<section number>* ↵

➠ **D**ot Leaders; **U**nderlining Allowed; **B**lank Line Between Authorities

➠ **F7** (Exit)

To generate a table of authorities:

Alt-F5 (Mark Text) *or* ⌨ **M**ark pull-down

➠ **G**enerate

➠ **G**enerate Tables, Indexes, Cross-References, etc.

➠ Existing tables, lists, and indexes will be replaced. Continue? **Y**es (**No**) ↵ *or any key except N*

USAGE
═══════════════════════════════

Tables of authorities are used in legal documents as lists of citations. Creating them involves essentially the same three steps as creating tables of contents: (1) marking the citations, (2) defining the style, and (3) generating the table.

You can divide a table of authorities into 16 sections, such as statutes, regulations, treaties, and so forth. Within each section, WordPerfect sorts the authorities alphanumerically.

Marking Citations
for a Table of Authorities

To mark citations for inclusion in a table of authorities:

1. Move to the beginning of the document. You can press Search (F2) or Extended Search (Home F2) and specify the citation you wish to find in the document, or simply move to the first occurrence of the citation.

2. Mark the first occurrence of the citation in its full form by highlighting the entire citation.

3. Press Alt-F5 (Mark Text) and select ToA, or choose Table of Authorities from the Mark menu; then choose Mark Full.

4. The following prompt appears:

   ToA Section Number (Press Enter for Short Form Only):

   For the first occurrence of the citation, enter the number of the section in which you want the citation to be listed in the table of authorities. If this is not the first occurrence and you have already defined a short form, simply press ⏎ to have WordPerfect mark the citation and its section number for you.

5. For the first occurrence of the citation, WordPerfect presents you with an editing screen in which you can edit the full form of the citation. The text can be up to 30 lines long, and you can use different character styles (bold, italics, and so forth), different fonts, and formats such as indentation.

6. When you have edited the full form of the citation, press Exit (F7). WordPerfect then presents you with a suggested short form (the first 40 characters of the full form) on the prompt line. You can shorten the short form even further or accept the program's suggestion by simply pressing ⏎. The short form must be unique for each citation.

7. Search for the next occurrence of the citation by using Search (F2) to move directly to it or press Home F2

to do an extended search through text, graphic boxes, footnotes, and endnotes.

8. When the program stops at the next occurrence of the citation, press Mark Text (Alt-F5) and select ToA Short Form. The program displays the short form you have defined. Press ↵ to accept it and mark the citation in the document, or choose Table of Authorities from the Mark menu; then choose Mark Short. (If no text is blocked, the Mark Full option will be in brackets.)

Defining the Style of a Table of Authorities

To define the style of a table of authorities:

1. Move the cursor to the location where you want the table of authorities to be generated, usually at the beginning of the document.

2. Press Ctrl-↵ to insert a hard page break. Renumber the first text page as page 1 so that references will be accurate. Position the cursor on the new page and type the heading you want for the table, such as **Table of Authorities**; press ↵ twice to move to a new line.

3. Define each section as you want it to be included in the table. Enter the section name (such as **CASES** or **STATUTES**). Press Alt-F6 (Flush Right) to align the heading *Page:* at the right margin, and enter **Page:**. Press ↵ to move to a new line to separate the heading from the entries that will be generated. Then press Mark Text (Alt-F5) and select Define, or choose Define from the Mark menu. Select Define Table of Authorities, enter the section number at the prompt, and press ↵.

4. Select the style you wish to use in that section from the options that appear. You can choose whether to use dot leaders, allow underlining, or allow space between citations. Press ↵ to return to the document.

5. Repeat steps 3 and 4 for each section.

If you don't start with a new page number between the definition of the table of authorities and the first text that has been marked for inclusion in the table, your page number references may not be accurate, and WordPerfect will warn you if it does not find a New Page Number code.

Generating a Table of Authorities

After you have marked text for your table of authorities and defined the style of the sections, you can generate the table itself, as shown in the step sequence.

The table will be generated at the [Def Mark] code where you defined the document. If your computer does not have sufficient RAM to hold the entire table in memory, you may be asked to close the Doc 2 window so that WordPerfect can use more memory for generating the table.

To delete a table of authorities, be sure to delete both the [Def Mark] code and the [End Def] code marking the end of the table. If WordPerfect finds a [Def Mark] code but no [End Def] code, it will continue to generate a table of authorities each time you generate your tables and lists.

Editing a Table of Authorities

To edit the full form of a citation in a table of authorities after you have generated the table, position the cursor to the right of the code for the full form in the Reveal Codes screen. Then select Define from the Mark Text menu (Alt-F5), and select Edit Table of Authorities Full Form. If you are using pull-down menus, select Table of Authorities from the Mark menu; then choose Edit Full.

The citation will be displayed on the screen. After you have edited it, press Exit (F7). Then enter the section number to which this citation belongs and press ↵.

You must then generate a new table of authorities to update the changes you have made.

SEE ALSO

Mark Text; Page Numbering.

Tables of Contents

Allows you to generate from entries in your document a table of contents that is automatically maintained by WordPerfect.

SEQUENCE OF STEPS

To mark an entry for the table of contents:

Alt-F4 (Block) *or* ⌐ᗺ **E**dit pull-down *then* **B**lock

➠ *[highlight text to be included]*

➠ **Alt-F5** (Mark Text) *or* ⌐ᗺ **M**ark pull-down

➠ To**C**

➠ ToC Level: *<level number between 1 and 5>* ↵

To define the style of the table of contents:

Alt-F5 (Mark Text) *or* ⌐ᗺ **M**ark pull-down

➠ **D**efine

➠ **D**efine Table of **C**ontents

➠ **N**umber of Levels *<1–5>*

➠ **D**isplay Last Level in Wrapped Format **N**o (**Y**es)

➠ **P**age Numbering (**N**one; **P**g # Follows; (Pg#) Follows; **F**lush Rt; Flush Rt with **L**eader) *[repeat for levels 1 through 5 as needed]*

➠ **F7** (Exit)

To generate a table of contents:

Alt-F5 (Mark Text) *or* ⌐ **M**ark pull-down

➠ **Generate**

➠ **Generate Tables, Indexes, Cross-References, etc.**

➠ **Existing tables, lists, and indexes will be replaced. Continue? Yes** (/**No**) ↵ *or any key except N*

USAGE

Creating a table of contents consists of three basic steps: (1) marking the headings, (2) defining the style, and (3) generating the table.

Marking Text for a Table of Contents

You can mark up to five levels of headings to be included in a table of contents. For each heading you want included in the table of contents, follow these steps:

1. Press Alt-F4 to mark the heading as a block.

2. Press Mark Text (Alt-F5). If you are using pull-down menus, choose Table of Contents from the Mark menu. The following prompt appears:

   Mark for: **1** To**C**; **2 L**ist; **3 I**ndex; **4** To**A**: 0

3. Select the ToC option. The following prompt appears:

   ToC Level:

4. Enter the level of the heading (from 1 to 5).

5. Repeat steps 1 through 4 for each item you want to include in the table of contents.

WordPerfect inserts [Mark] and [End Mark] codes around each entry as you mark it. To remove the markings so that an

item will not be included in the table of contents, delete the
[Mark] code.

Defining the Style
of a Table of Contents

When you define the style of a table of contents, WordPerfect
creates the table at that point in your document. For this
reason, go to the beginning of your document, press Ctrl-⏎
to create a new, blank page, and type any heading you may
want for the contents page, such as **Contents**. Then press ⏎
to add space between the heading and the table entries that
will be generated at that point.

To define the format of the contents page (required before
you can generate a table of contents):

1. Press Mark Text (Alt-F5) and select the Define option. If
   you are using pull-down menus, select Define from the
   Mark menu.

2. Select Define Table of Contents. The Table of Contents
   Definition screen appears.

3. Select Number of Levels and enter the number of heading levels you are using in the table of contents (1–5).

4. Select Display Last Level in Wrapped Format and type **Y**
   if you want the last level of entries to be wrapped on one
   line, rather than listed vertically. If you enter **Y**, Word-
   Perfect displays the headings with the last level as one
   wrapped line and the headings and page numbers separated by semicolons. The default is No.

5. Select Page Numbering Position and enter a numbering
   style for each level. Choose option **1** or **N** to print headings only, with no page numbers. If you choose option **2**
   or **3** (or **P** or **(**), page numbers will occur next to headings,
   and with option **3** or **(**, they will be in parentheses.
   Options **4** and **5** (or **F** and **L**) place page numbers flush
   right, with or without dot leaders.

Generating a Table of Contents

After you have marked text for your table of contents, created a page for it, and defined its style, you can generate the table itself, as shown in the sequence of steps.

The table will be generated at the [Def Mark] code where you defined the document. If your computer does not have sufficient RAM to hold the entire table in memory, you may be asked to close the Doc 2 window so that WordPerfect can use more of the memory for generating the table.

To delete a table of contents, be sure to delete both the [Def Mark] code and the [End Def] code marking the end of the table. If WordPerfect finds a [Def Mark] code but no [End Def] code, it will continue to generate a table of contents each time you generate your tables and lists.

If you edit your document so that page breaks change, be sure to generate a new table of contents. WordPerfect does not automatically update tables of contents as page changes occur.

SEE ALSO

Cross-Reference; Lists; Mark Text.

Tabs

Allows you to change the tab settings in your document.

SEQUENCE OF STEPS

To enter equally spaced tabs:

Shift-F8 (Format) *or* ⌐ Layout pull-down

➠ **Line**

➠ **Tab Set**

➠ *<start position>,<increment spacing>* ↵

➠ **F7 F7** (Exit)

To clear all tabs and set different kinds of tabs individually:

Shift-F8 (Format) *or* ⌨ Layout pull-down

➠ **L**ine

➠ **T**ab Set

➠ **Ctrl-End** (Delete End of line)

➠ *[move cursor to desired position(s) on ruler]*

➠ **T**ype; **L**eft; **R**ight; **D**ecimal; **.** = Dot Leader

➠ **F7 F7** (Exit)

USAGE

WordPerfect is preset with left-justified tabs every ½ inch up to position 8.5". To move to the next tab setting, use the Tab key.

To set individual tabs, select Format, then Line. Select Tab Set and the Tab Set menu will appear. To select a new tab stop, move the cursor to the position on the ruler line where you want the new tab and type **L** for a left-justified tab, **R** for a right-justified tab, **C** for a centered tab, **D** for a decimal tab, or **.** (period) for a dot-leader tab. You can indicate that dot leaders be used with left, right, or decimal tabs by moving the cursor to the L, R, or C tab that has already been set and typing a period. As you type, when you press Tab and the next tab has been set as a dot-leader tab, you will see the dot leaders appear on your screen.

Table 7 illustrates the various types of tabs you can set.

You may use the space bar or the → key to position the cursor on the tab ruler line to see where these tabs appear in relation to your text. You can also type the number of the position where you want a tab and press ↵. For example, to set a tab at the 6.3" mark, type **6.3** and press ↵. In Word-Perfect 5.1, you can determine whether tabs are relative to the left margin (the default) or an absolute distance from the left margin, as in WordPerfect 5.0. An absolute (or "hard") tab will remain in the same position even when you change margin settings; the tab ruler shows it as a distance from the left edge of the page. In version 5.1, tabs are relative—that is, they remain in place relative to the left margin so that even when you change the left margin, a tab set as +1 remains one inch from the left margin. To change the type of tab from relative to absolute, select Type from the tab ruler menu; then choose Absolute. You can also enter hard tabs in version 5.1 in the following way:

To Enter	Press	Code
Hard Left	Home Tab	[TAB]
Hard Right	Home Alt-F6	[RGT TAB]
Hard Center	Home Shift-F6	[CNTR TAB]
Hard Decimal	Ctrl-F6	[DEC TAB]

To delete the existing tabs and set new ones, press Home Home ← to move to the beginning of the line; then press Ctrl-End to delete the existing tab settings. You do not need to delete old tab settings before you set new ones, however.

TAB TYPE	HOW SET	EXAMPLE
Left-justified	L	First Quarter `.......L............`
Right-justified	R	First Quarter `............R............`
Centered	C	First Quarter `..............C..........`
Decimal	D	$1,256.00 `...........D............`
Dot-leader left	L	Benefits.........Section 1.11 `L................L...........`
Dot-leader right	R	Benefits...Section 1.11 `L....................R.....`
Dot-leader decimal	D	Benefits.....Section 1.11 `L....................D.....`

Table 7: Types of Tabs

To delete a single tab, move to the setting on the line; then press Backspace or Delete.

To return to your document without setting tabs after you have displayed the Tab Set menu, press Cancel (F1).

Setting Evenly Spaced Tabs

You can also specify that WordPerfect set tabs in evenly spaced increments. To do so, select Line from the Format menu, then select Tab Set. Move the cursor to the beginning of the line, and press Ctrl-End to delete the existing tab settings. Then move the cursor to the first tab stop that you want to set and type **L**, **R**, **C**, or **D** to establish the style of the evenly spaced tabs you are setting (left, right, centered, or decimal). If you are using the default of left-justified tabs, you do not have to take this step.

Then type the number of the character position where you want tabs to start, type a comma, then type the increment by which you want them to be spaced. Finally, press Exit (F7) twice to return to the document.

For example, to set decimal tabs every inch starting one inch from the left margin, you would type **D** at the 1" position and then type **1,1** and press ↵.

SEE ALSO

Tab Align.

Text In/Out

Allows you to retrieve a DOS text (ASCII) file into WordPerfect; to save a document as a DOS text, generic, WordPerfect 5.0, or WordPerfect 4.2 file; to create document comments; and to assign passwords to documents.

SEQUENCE OF STEPS

To retrieve a DOS text file:

Ctrl-F5 (Text In/Out) *then* DOS **T**ext *then* **R**etrieve
(CR/LF to HRt); **R**etrieve (CR/LF to SRt in HZone)

or ⌐ **F**ile pull-down *then* Text **I**n *then* DOS Text
(CR/LF to **H**Rt); DOS Text (CR/LF to **S**Rt)

➥ *<file name>* ↵

To save a DOS text file:

Ctrl-F5 (Text In/Out) *or* ⌐ **F**ile pull-down *then*
Text **O**ut

➥ **D**OS Text

➥ **S**ave *[Specify file name]*

To save a document as generic, WordPerfect 5.0, or Word-
Perfect 4.2 format:

Ctrl-F5 (Text In/Out) *then* Save **A**s

or ⌐ **F**ile pull-down *then* Text **o**ut

➥ **G**eneric; **W**ordPefect 5.0; WordPerfect 4.2

➥ *<file name>* ↵

Note: The Text In/Out options are slightly different in
WordPerfect 5.0. The Save As options are listed on the Text
In/Out menu (Ctrl-F5) as Save **G**eneric or Save **W**P 4.2. In
addition, you can retrieve DOS text files from the List Files
screen (F5) with **T**ext In, which is no longer possible in version 5.1, as that option has been replaced by Short/Long
Display.

USAGE

The Text In/Out option allows you to bring DOS text files
into WordPerfect, to save WordPerfect documents in DOS
text file format, to assign password protection to files (see
Locking a File), to save WordPerfect 5.0 and 5.1 files in

earlier WordPerfect formats, to save WordPerfect documents in a generic word processor format, and to create document comments (see **Document Comments**). In version 5.1, a new option, Spreadsheet, allows you to import spreadsheet files by using this menu (see **Spreadsheet**).

Importing and Exporting DOS Text Files

To convert a document to DOS text file (ASCII) format within WordPerfect, use the DOS Text option on the Text In/Out menu (Ctrl-F5). If you are using pull-down menus, select Text Out from the File menu. When you select Save with the keyboard menu or DOS Text with the pull-down menu, you will be prompted for a file name for the DOS text file. In this format, most of the codes that WordPerfect uses to control formatting are removed. Some WordPerfect codes that control indenting, centering, paragraph numbering, and the Date function are converted to ASCII codes, however. All of your document except footnotes and endnotes will be converted.

To retrieve a document that is in DOS text file format, use one of the Retrieve options on the Text In/Out menu instead of using the Retrieve command (Shift-F10). If you are using pull-down menus, select Text In from the File menu. You can choose whether carriage returns and line feeds in the DOS text document are converted to hard returns (CR/LF to [HRt]) in WordPerfect, so you get a line-for-line conversion. If you are bringing in data or lines of programming code for which you want to use WordPerfect as a text editor, choose this option, which preserves the column and row format. You may also want to set your margins wider before you import the document to make sure that wide rows are kept intact. (For additional information if you are bringing in data from a database program to use in mail-merge operations, see **Merge Operations**; if you are bringing in data from a spreadsheet program such as Lotus 1-2-3, see **Spreadsheet**.)

If you choose DOS Text (CR/LF to SRt), carriage returns and line feeds in the DOS text document are converted to soft returns when they occur in the hyphenation zone, so hard returns will not occur in the middle of a paragraph in the imported document. You should use this option for word-wrapped text. You may want to set your margins in WordPerfect as close as possible to those of the DOS text file so that the same line breaks occur.

In WordPerfect 5.0, you can also use the Text In option on the List Files menu (F5) to retrieve DOS text files. It is the same as the Retrieve (CR/LF to [HRt]) option on the Text In/Out menu.

Converting Documents to Other Word Processor Formats

If you are using pull-down menus in WordPerfect 5.1, the Text Out option allows you to save them as Generic (in generic word processing format), as WordPerfect 5.0 documents, or as WordPerfect 4.2 documents. If you are not using pull-down menus, choose Save As from the Text In/Out menu (Ctrl-F5) and then select the format you want. WordPerfect 5.0, of course, provides only the Generic and 4.2 options.

In generic word processing format, special WordPerfect format codes are not saved, but the overall text format is maintained. Footnotes and endnotes are not converted, however. In place of the codes that indicate centering, indenting, flush-right text, and soft returns, spaces are inserted, and <CR><LF> (carriage return–line feed) codes are inserted in place of hard returns.

If you convert WordPerfect 5.0 or 5.1 documents to an earlier version of WordPerfect, be sure to use a different name from that of the current document so that you do not overwrite it.

If you are converting 5.1 documents to 5.0 format, the codes for the features that are new in version 5.1 will be removed from the document.

You can retrieve a document that was created in WordPerfect version 5.1 into WordPerfect version 5.0. Codes that version 5.0 does not recognize will be shown as [Unknown].

If you are converting 5.0 documents to 4.2 format, you should be aware that some 4.2 codes, such as font change codes, do not have equivalents in version 5.0. If you have such codes in your 5.0 document, you can use a special file called STANDARD.CRS to manually change the codes.

SEE ALSO

Document Comments; List Files; Locking a File; Merge Operations; Printing to Disk; Spreadsheet.

Thesaurus

Allows you to look for synonyms for any word in the text of your document.

SEQUENCE OF STEPS

[position cursor on word to be looked up]

➠ **Alt-F1** (Thesaurus) *or* ⌐ **T**ools pull-down *then* **T**hesaurus

➠ **1** Replace Word; **2** View Doc; **3** Look Up Word; **4** Clear Column

USAGE

On a floppy disk system, you must first insert the Thesaurus disk into drive B. (Note: WordPerfect 5.1 requires that each of your floppy disk drives be 720K or higher.) Since Word-Perfect normally looks for the Thesaurus on the default drive, this means you must also change the Thesaurus default drive to B by using the Setup menu. When you have finished using the Thesaurus, replace your data disk in drive B and save any changes. On a hard disk system, the Thesaurus is installed in the default directory during the installation process, and no special instructions are needed.

There are several ways to look up a word:

- Move the cursor to the word in your document and press Thesaurus (Alt-F1).

- If you are already in the Thesaurus, select View Doc, move the cursor to the word you want to look up, and press Thesaurus (Alt-F1).

- If the word you want to look up is not displayed on the screen, press Alt-F1 (to start the Thesaurus), select Look Up Word, and then enter the word.

While you are using the Thesaurus, you will see a few lines of your document at the top of the screen, along with three columns of alternatives, grouped into nouns, verbs, adjectives, and adverbs, as well as antonyms—words of opposite meaning. Any word preceded by a dot is a *headword*, which indicates that you can look up further references to that word by pressing the accompanying letter. At the bottom of the screen is a menu that allows you to replace words, view more of your document, and look up other words.

Replacing a Word

Replace Word allows you to replace the highlighted word in your document with any of the suggested words (with accompanying letters) that appear on the Thesaurus screen. You can move between the columns of words by using the ← and → keys; the letters will follow the cursor, allowing you to select more words. The ↑ and ↓ keys as well as the PgUp and PgDn keys scroll the columns vertically. The Home Home ↑ and Home Home ↓ key combinations take you to the beginning and end of the Thesaurus entry.

To view groups of related words, type the letter corresponding to any of the headwords (those with dots to their left).

Viewing a Document

The View Doc option allows you to return to view your document—for example, to get a better idea of the context in which the word was used. When you are in the document, you can use the cursor movement keys to scroll through the text. After using View Doc, you can return to the Thesaurus screen you were viewing before by pressing Exit (F7), or you can press Alt-F1 again to look up another word in the Thesaurus.

Looking Up a Word

Look Up Word directs the Thesaurus to look up a word. WordPerfect will prompt you to enter the word you want to look up.

Clearing a Column

If your screen becomes cluttered with too many alternative words, you can use the Clear Column option to clear the column the cursor is in to make room for more synonyms of another headword.

SEE ALSO

Speller.

Typeover

Toggles between the default Insert mode and Typeover mode.

SEQUENCE OF STEPS

Ins

USAGE

WordPerfect is preset for Insert mode, which means that characters you type are inserted on the screen, with existing characters being pushed to the right of the cursor. To use Typeover mode, in which characters you type replace the characters on the screen, press Ins. A *Typeover* message appears at the bottom of the screen when Typeover is on. To return to Insert mode, press Ins again.

Pressing Tab in Typeover mode does not insert a tab but simply moves the cursor to the next tab stop.

To define a macro in which the typing mode changes, use WordPerfect's Forced Typeover mode (Home Ins) or Forced Insert mode (Home Home Ins). Otherwise, each time you execute the macro, WordPerfect will use the mode you were in when you recorded the macro.

Type Through (Version 5.0)

Allows you to use your printer as a typewriter so that any character or line you type is immediately printed. This feature is not available in version 5.1.

SEQUENCE OF STEPS

Shift-F7 (Print)

➡ **Ty**pe Through

➡ **L**ine; **C**haracter

➡ *<characters or line>*

➡ **F7** (Exit)

USAGE

WordPerfect's Type Through feature (version 5.0) allows you to use your keyboard as you would a typewriter. The text you type is not saved, however, but is sent directly to the printer, so you need to position the paper so that the printhead is on the first line to be printed.

To use the Type Through feature, press Shift-F7 and choose Type Through. Then select By Line or By Character. Use the By Line option if you want the characters you type to be sent to the printer only when you press ⏎. Choose the

By Character option if you want each character to go to the printer as it is typed; remember, however, that you cannot correct characters if you use this option.

When you use Type Through, you are placed in a special Type Through screen. The line at the top of the screen displays the previously typed line. You cannot edit it, but if you press Move (Ctrl-F4) it will be copied to the bottom line, which can be edited. You can enter up to 200 characters per line; lines that are too wide to be displayed on the screen will move to the left as you type.

While in Type Through mode, you can use the space bar to move the cursor to the right. You can also use the arrow keys to move the cursor right or left, and Home with the → or ← key moves the cursor to the beginning or end of a line. Pressing Format (Shift-F8) allows you to insert printer command codes. Press Exit (F7) or Cancel (F1) to return to the regular editing screen.

Undelete

Restores any of the last three deletions at the cursor's position.

SEQUENCE OF STEPS

F1 (Cancel) *or* ꗈ **E**dit pull-down *then* **U**ndelete

➠ **R**estore; **P**revious Deletion

USAGE

If WordPerfect is not carrying out a command, the Cancel key (F1) functions as an Undelete key. You can also select Undelete from the Edit menu, if you are using pull-down menus. The following prompt appears along with the most recently deleted text:

Undelete: **1 R**estore; **2 P**revious Deletion: 0

Choosing Restore restores the displayed text to your document; choosing Previous Deletion displays the text that was deleted prior to that deletion. Three levels of deletions can be displayed and restored. After the third most recently deleted text is displayed, selecting Previous Deletion displays the first deletion again. Selecting Restore restores the displayed deletion to your document.

SEE ALSO

Cancel.

Underline

Underscores selected portions of text.

SEQUENCE OF STEPS

To underline new text:

F8 (Underline) *or* ⌐⊐ **F**ont pull-down *then*
Appearance *then* **U**nderline

⫸ *<text to be underlined>*

⫸ **F8** (Underline) or →

To underline existing text:

F4 (Block)

⫸ *[highlight text to be underlined]*

⫸ **F8** Underline *or* ⌐⊐ **F**ont pull-down *then*
Appearance *then* **U**nderline

USAGE

To underline new text, press F8 before you type. After you press F8, the Pos indicator appears underlined, indicating that text you type will be underlined. To turn underlining off, press F8 again. You can indicate a block of existing text to be underlined (by pressing Alt-F4 and marking the block). You can also select Appearance from the Font pull-down menu; then select Underline.

You can also underline text by pressing Font (Ctrl-F8), selecting Appearance, and selecting Undrln.

WordPerfect is preset to underline spaces between words but not spaces created by pressing the Tab key. To change these settings, choose Other from the Format menu (Shift-F8); then select Underline.

To use double underlining in a document, press Font (Ctrl-F8), select Appearance, and then select Double Underline. You will not see the double underline on the screen unless you have a graphics card such as the Hercules Graphics Card Plus, but it will appear in your document when it is printed.

SEE ALSO

Font: Changing the Appearance of the Font.

View Document

Allows you to preview the way the document will appear when printed.

SEQUENCE OF STEPS

Shift-F7 (Print) *or* ▭ **F**ile pull-down *then* **P**rint

➠ **V**iew Document

➠ **1** 100%; **2** 200%; **3** Full Page; **4** Facing Pages

➠ **F7** (Exit)

USAGE

Choosing View Document from the Print menu allows you to see how your document will appear when it is printed, complete with text elements that are not normally visible on the screen, such as page numbers and headers. You can select the 100% option to view the document in its actual size, 200% to see it at twice its actual size, or Full Page to view the page. If you select the Facing Pages option, you will see odd-numbered pages on the right and even-numbered pages on the left.

Once you have displayed a page or pages, you can use the cursor movement keys to scroll through the document, or use the PgUp, PgDn, Screen Up, and Screen Down keys.

To see the previewed pages in reverse video, press Switch (Shift-F3) while you are in the View Document screen.

To return to your document after previewing it, press Exit (F7).

SEE ALSO

Graphics.

Widow/Orphan Protection

Prevents either the first or last line of a paragraph from being separated from the rest of the paragraph by a soft page break.

SEQUENCE OF STEPS

Shift-F8 (Format) *or* ⌐▭ **Layout** pull-down

➠ **Line**

➠ **Widow/Orphan Protection Y** *or* **N**

➠ **F7** (Exit)

USAGE

Widow/Orphan protection instructs the program not to leave the first line of text in a paragraph by itself as the last line of a page (a widow) or the last line of a paragraph as the first line of a page (an orphan). Widow lines are forced to the next page, while orphan lines get one more line added from the previous page.

To turn on Widow/Orphan protection for an entire document, move the cursor to the beginning. Select Format and then the Line option. Select Widow/Orphan Protection and enter **Y**. This option is a toggle; to turn off Widow/Orphan protection, type **N**.

SEE ALSO

Block Protect; Conditional End of Page; Page Break, Soft and Hard.

Windows

Allows you to split the editing screen into two windows in order to view the text in the Doc 1 and Doc 2 editing areas simultaneously.

SEQUENCE OF STEPS

Ctrl-F3 (Screen) *or* ⟍⊟⟍ **E**dit pull-down

▥➡ **Window**

▥➡ **Number of lines in this window:** *<number>*
    ↵ *or* ↑/↓ ↵

USAGE

To split the screen into two windows, select Window from the Screen key menu or the Edit pull-down menu. Word-Perfect will prompt you for the number of lines of text you want to see in the current window. The screen can display up to 24 lines, so you can enter any combination that adds up to 24. For example, to see 12 lines in each window, enter **12**; to see 18 lines in one window and 6 in the other, enter **18**.

You can also use the ↑ and ↓ keys to move the cursor to the position where you want the split to occur and then press ↵. The window will be split at the cursor position.

To move back and forth between windows, press Switch (Shift-F3), or choose Switch Document from the Edit pull-down menu. To remove the split screen and return to a full-screen display, press Ctrl-F3, select Window, and this time enter **0** or **24** as the number of lines you want displayed. The second document will still be in memory, and you can return to it at any time by pressing Switch (Shift-F3).

You can view the same document in each of the two windows by retrieving it into both windows—for example, if you want to see the beginning and end of a long document at the same time. Both documents will have the same file name, however, so you will have to keep track of which version you want to have as the final saved version.

SEE ALSO

Switch Document.

Word/Letter Spacing

Allows you to adjust the spacing between letters of a word and/or between words in a line.

SEQUENCE OF STEPS

Shift-F8 (Format) *or* ⌐ **L**ayout pull-down

➠ **O**ther

➠ **P**rinter Functions

➠ **W**ord Spacing/Letter Spacing

➠ **Word Spacing: N**ormal; **O**ptimal; **P**ercent of Optimal ↵; **S**et Pitch ↵

➠ Letter Spacing: **N**ormal; **O**ptimal; **P**ercent of Optimal; **4 S**et Pitch

➠ **F7** (Exit)

USAGE

WordPerfect's Word/Letter Spacing option allows you to adjust the spacing between words and between letters within words. When you justify text, for example, you may want to adjust the amount of space that the program adds between words to make the line of text come out even with the right margin. Letter spacing is normally used to add spaces between letters, creating a visual effect that is widely seen in company logos and on business cards, for example. In its opposite, called kerning, the amount of space between letters is reduced.

To change the word or letter spacing, select Format (or choose Other from the Layout pull-down menu) and select Other. Next select Printer Functions and choose Word Spacing/Letter Spacing from the menu that appears. You can then select a setting for word spacing, letter spacing, or both.

The Normal setting sets spacing between words as well as letters to the amount recommended by the manufacturer of your printer. Optimal, which is the default, produces the setting that appears best according to the manufacturer of WordPerfect. The Optimal and Normal settings are often, but not always, the same.

If you want to specify the amount of space to be used between words and letters, choose Percent of Optimal and enter a percentage. Percentages less than 100% reduce the amount of space, while percentages greater than 100% enlarge it. Normally, you will not want to change the default setting unless you want to create special typographic effects.

If you want to adjust the spacing between words and letters in terms of pitch (characters per inch), use the Set Pitch option and enter the pitch you want to use. WordPerfect then calculates the correct Percent of Optimal setting needed to generate that pitch in the font you are currently using.

SEE ALSO

Justification; Kerning; Leading.

Index